Exploring
America
in the 1970s

Exploring
America
in the 1970s

Celebrating the Self

**Molly Sandling &
Kimberley L. Chandler, Ph.D.**

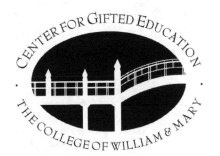

CENTER FOR GIFTED EDUCATION

THE COLLEGE OF WILLIAM & MARY

The College of William and Mary
School of Education
Center for Gifted Education
P.O. Box 8795
Williamsburg, VA 23187

Prufrock Press Inc.
P.O. Box 8813
Waco, TX 76714-8813
Phone: (800) 998-2208
Fax: (800) 240-0333
http://www.prufrock.com

Contents

Acknowledgement

Thanks to Pamela N. Harris, who acted as the editorial assistant for this unit.

Unit Overview

Introduction to the *Exploring America* Units

These humanities units will focus on the way in which the literature, art, and music of each decade reflect the history and events that were occurring in America at that time. These units are intended to stimulate student interest and creativity, to develop higher order thinking skills, and to promote interdisciplinary learning.

The units could be used as a supplement to a social studies curriculum or a language arts curriculum, or could be used as stand-alone materials in a gifted education program.

Introduction to *Exploring America in the 1970s: Celebrating the Self*

Exploring America in the 1970s: Celebrating the Self is about Americans expressing their individuality and confronting a new identity as the legacy of the Civil Rights Movement allowed other groups to express their pride and heritage, the situation in Vietnam altered our confidence, and tensions began to increase in the Middle East. Topics included in the unit are:

» the music about economic struggles and the emotions felt by Americans during the hard economic times of the 1970s;

- » the Women's Liberation Movement and the debate over the Equal Rights Amendment (ERA);
- » the music, murals, and poetry of the growing Chicano Movement;
- » songs and documents surrounding the American Indian Movement and its protests during the 1970s;
- » literature and music capturing the emotions of African Americans in the post-Civil Rights era;
- » the accuracy of the "melting pot" label in contrast to the emphasis on self-help and the "me decade;"
- » reactions to Watergate and the Oil Crisis;
- » songs and other cultural creations to celebrate the Bicentennial of the United States; and
- » disco music and its significance and role in the 1970s.

Standards Alignment

Social Studies

This unit includes activities that address the National Council for the Social Studies National Curriculum Standards for Social Studies. Specifically, the activities relate to all 10 themes of the National Curriculum Standards for Social Studies: Culture; Time, Continuity, and Change; People, Places, and Environments; Individual, Development, and Identity; Individuals, Groups, and Institutions; Power, Authority, and Governance; Production, Distribution, and Consumption; Science, Technology, and Society; Global Connections; and Civic Ideals and Practices.

English/Language Arts

This unit also includes activities that align to these Anchor Standards of the Common Core State Standards (CCSS) in English/language arts:
- » CCSS.ELA-Literacy.CCRA.R.1: Read closely to determine what the text says explicitly and to make logical inferences from it; cite specific textual evidence when writing or speaking to support conclusions drawn from the text.
- » CCSS.ELA-Literacy.CCRA.R.2: Determine central ideas or themes of a text and analyze their development; summarize the key supporting details and ideas.
- » CCSS.ELA-Literacy.CCRA.R.4: Interpret words and phrases as they are used in a text, including determining technical, connotative, and figurative meanings, and analyze how specific word choices shape meaning or tone.
- » CCSS.ELA-Literacy.CCRA.R.7: Integrate and evaluate content presented in diverse media and formats, including visually and quantitatively, as well as in words.
- » CCSS.ELA-Literacy.CCRA.R.9: Analyze how two or more texts address similar themes or topics in order to build knowledge or to compare the approaches the authors take.
- » CCSS.ELA-Literacy.CCRA.R.10: Read and comprehend complex literary and informational texts independently and proficiently.

Overarching Concept

The overarching concept for this unit is *identity*. This concept can help students to understand events, music, art, and literature during the 1970s. The unit explores the decade, giving students multiple opportunities to analyze events based on a developing understanding of how the idea of identity applies to specific situations. The conceptual approach also allows students the opportunity to make comparisons to other time periods, thus developing a deeper understanding of the generalizations about identity and when they may or may not apply.

The first lesson in this unit introduces the concept of identity. Teachers may wish to conduct an activity based on Hilda Taba's (1962) Concept Development Model prior to teaching the first lesson. Students are asked to brainstorm examples of identity, categorize their examples, identify "nonexamples" of the concept, and make generalizations about the concept. The following generalizations about identity are incorporated into this unit of study:

» Identity changes with new ideas, experiences, conditions, or in response to other expressions of identity.

» Identity is created by a group, person, or outsiders, and self-created identities may be different from how others see one's self.

» There are multiple elements of identity and at different times, different elements have greater or lesser importance.

» Although members of a group or society may have different individual identities, they still share particular elements of identity.

Identity is integrated throughout unit lessons and deepens students' understanding of social studies and a given historical period. Students examine the relationship of important ideas, abstractions, and issues through the application of the concept "generalizations."

Curriculum Framework

Concept Goal

Goal 1: To understand the concept of identity in 1970s America. Students will be able to:

» describe how the American identity changed during the 1970s; and

» describe how changes in American identity in the 1970s were revealed in the music, art, and literature of the decade.

Process Goals

Goal 2: To develop skills in historical analysis and song and artwork interpretation. Students will be able to:

» define the context in which a song or piece of art was produced and the implications of context for understanding the artifact;

» describe a writer's or artist's intent in producing a given song or piece of art based on understanding of text and context;

» consider short- and long-term consequences of a given document or artifact; and

» analyze the effects of given documents or artifacts on the interpretation of historical events.

Goal 3: To develop analytical and interpretive skills in literature. Students will be able to:

» describe what a selected literary passage means;

» cite similarities and differences in meaning among selected works of literature; and

» make inferences based on information in given passages.

Content Goal

Goal 4: To develop an understanding of historical events occurring in the United States during the 1970s. Students will be able to:

» describe major historical events during the 1970s that affected the American identity; and

» describe music, art, and literature of the 1970s that reflected the American identity.

Assessing Student Learning

Teachers should assess student progress based on the quality of individual products and achievement toward the goals of the unit. Question responses should be assessed based on demonstration of insight and ability to use text to support inferences. Writing activities should be assessed based on understanding of the social studies content, and may also be assessed for clarity and insight as desired. Oral presentations of completed work should be assessed based on coherence, content, and clarity of the presentation. Teachers may provide rubrics for students related to the required assignments or work with students to develop rubrics for assessment.

Teaching Resources

Recommended History Books

These history textbooks are recommended for providing supplementary information about the historical background of the events described in this unit.

Appleby, J. (2010). *American vision*. New York, NY: Glencoe/McGraw Hill.

Cayton, A. R. L., Perry, E. I., Reed, L., & Winkler, A. M. (2002). *Pathways to the present*. Upper Saddle Ridge, NJ: Pearson Prentice Hall.

Davidson, J. W., Stoff, M. B., & Viola, H. J. (2002). *The American nation*. Upper Saddle Ridge, NJ: Pearson Prentice Hall.

Kennedy, D. M., & Cohen, L. (2012). *The American pageant*. Boston, MA: Cengage Learning.

Useful Websites

» *American Experience: Eyes on the Prize*:
   http://www.pbs.org/wgbh/amex/eyesontheprize

» *Chicano! History of the Mexican American Civil Rights Movement*:
   http://www.youtube.com/watch?v=NL4rQHKza9Y.

» Kurt Vonnegut website:
   http://www.vonnegut.com

» Library of Congress Civil Rights Resources:
   http://www.loc.gov/teachers/classroommaterials/themes/civil-rights

» Library of Congress Song and Poetry Analysis Tools:
   http://www.loc.gov/teachers/lyrical/tools

» National Archives Document Repository and Teaching Activities:
   http://docsteach.org/home/70s

» National Park Service, Historic Places of the Civil Rights Movement:
   http://www.cr.nps.gov/nr/travel/civilrights

» PBS Learning Media, Civil Rights:
   http://www.teachersdomain.org/special/civil

» PBS Makers: Women Who Make America:
   http://www.pbs.org/makers/home

» Rock and Roll Hall of Fame Education:
   http://www.rockhall.com/education

» Smithsonian Folkways:
   http://www.folkways.si.edu

» VH1 Music Studio:
   http://www.vh1.com/partners/vh1_music_studio/

Implementation Guide

This guide assists the teacher in implementing this unit in his or her classroom. It also includes background information about the instructional models utilized throughout the unit.

Guidelines

The following pages offer some general suggestions to help the teacher implement the unit effectively.

Support for Teachers Implementing the Unit

It is important for teachers implementing this unit to read it in depth before beginning instruction. Conferences and training workshops sponsored through the Center for Gifted Education (CFGE) can help teachers understand the core components of the unit and provide informal tips for teaching it. Customized professional development, including comprehensive curriculum planning for incorporating this humanities series, is also available. Please contact the CFGE at cfgepd@wm.edu for information about professional development options.

Suggested Grade Levels

Exploring America in the 1970s was designed for use with high-ability students in grades 6–8. Although the unit was developed for middle school students, some components may work well with students at other grade levels. Caution should be exercised when using the materials with elementary-aged students, however, as some of the music and literature contains mature themes.

How to Incorporate the Unit Within the Existing Social Studies Curriculum

This unit is intended to represent 5–8 weeks of instruction in social studies for high-ability learners. The unit may be taught as core content, or it may be used as a supplement to the core curriculum. The unit is also appropriate for use in a seminar setting.

Implementation Time

In this unit, a lesson is defined as at least two 2-hour sessions. A minimum of 40 instructional hours should be allocated for teaching the entire unit. Teachers are encouraged to extend the amount of time spent on the various topics included in the book based on available time and student interest.

Materials

Availability of materials. Given that this unit focuses on the 1970s decade, the materials are contemporary in nature and have not yet become part of the public domain. In most cases, it is suggested that teachers make use of Internet resources whenever possible rather than purchasing the materials cited. Both Prufrock Press and the Center for Gifted Education have developed websites that include a list of resources and their respective URLs: http://www.prufrock. com/Assets/ClientPages/exploring1970.aspx and http://education.wm.edu/centers/cfge/1970s. Because URLs tend to change, these websites will be updated periodically.

Potentially controversial materials. This unit focuses on the trends and issues in 1970s America. Some topics being discussed and some of the materials being used may be controversial to some students and parents. It is crucial that teachers preview all materials prior to teaching the unit and determine what is appropriate for their own schools and classrooms.

Teachers should always read the literature selections or listen to the musical selections before assigning them to students and be aware of what the school and/or district policy is on the use of materials that may be deemed controversial. Although many gifted readers are able to read books at a significantly higher Lexile level than what other children their age are reading, content that is targeted at older audiences may not be appropriate for them.

☐   Made original, insightful contribution(s) to discussion?

☐   Extended or elaborated on a classmate's ideas?

☐   Used evidence from the text or another student's comments to support ideas?

☐   Synthesized information from discussion in a meaningful way?

☐   Posed questions that enhanced the discussion and led to more in-depth understanding?

Student comments: _____

_____

_____

Teacher comments: _____

_____

_____

Figure 1. Participation checklist. Adapted from Center for Gifted Education (2011).

Assessment

This unit includes both formative and summative assessments, which are listed at the end of each lesson plan. Because discussion plays a prominent role in the students' learning in this unit, teachers may want to consider teaching students a specific process for the discussion elements and develop tools for assessing student participation. The Socratic Seminar is one method for organizing discussions. (See http://socraticseminars.com/socratic-seminars/ or http://www.readwritethink.org/professional-development/strategy-guides/socratic-seminars-30600.html for additional information.) Or, the teacher may want to design a checklist, such as the one in Figure 1, to give to students to keep track of their contributions during discussions. The students can check off the criteria as they meet them. Using this checklist, the student and teacher can monitor the student's participation in various discussions.

Teaching Models

There are five teaching models that are used in the unit to facilitate student achievement toward the unit objectives. Teachers should familiarize themselves with these models before beginning the unit.

The models are designed to promote discussions in various settings. The teacher should determine the best way of organizing students for discussion in order to facilitate student understanding and appreciation for the variety of answers that are given. These teaching models also provide students with the opportunity to support their responses with evidence from the literature or other resources. Multiple perspectives can be shared and encouraged through appropriate use of the models. The models also may be used to prepare students for a discussion in another content area or about a current event. Students can complete the models in a whole group, in small groups, or individually before or as they engage in a discussion. Varying the group size and group composition will provide students with many perspectives for consideration. For more information, see Center for Gifted Education (2011).

The models are listed below and described in the pages that follow.

1. Identity Chart
2. Literature Analysis Model
3. Primary Source Document Analysis Model
4. Music Analysis Model
5. Art Analysis Model

Identity Chart

The Identity Chart (see Figure 2) allows students to consider the concept of identity as they study the events of the mid-20th century and examine the effect of those events on the American identity. Some scholars (Huntington, 2004; Smith, 2010) have defined the elements that comprise identity; for purposes of this unit, these include:

»   time and place,
»   history and myths,
»   culture and traditions,
»   race and ethnicity,
»   civic identity,
»   international role, and
»   economy.

Prior to the first lesson, you may have students develop a list of the elements that they believe are part of the American identity, and then compare it to the one listed here. Have students determine the definition of each element and give examples.

Tell students that in this unit, they will be examining the American identity in the 1970s, trying to get a better understanding of why Americans interacted as they did. Explain that identity is important because it shapes our actions and interactions with others. Have students answer the following questions on their own, then debrief in the large group:

»   Do all of the elements of identity that we listed affect your actions equally at all times? Explain your answer.
»   Sometimes various elements of identity are emphasized more than others. What are some examples? Why does this happen?
»   When is each of these elements most important? Least important? Why?
»   Which elements are most influential on your actions when you are at school? When you go on vacation? When you meet someone new? When you have to make an important decision? Why?

Explain that the questions and responses just discussed address individual (personal) identity. Have students answer the following questions:

»   What other types of identity are there?
»   How can a group's identity be different from an individual's identity within that group?

HANDOUT

Identity Chart

Identity	Time and Place
	Culture and Traditions
	History and Myths
	International Role
	Economy
	Civic Identity
	Race/Ethnicity

Figure 2. Identity Chart.

This discussion serves as the initial one regarding identity, specifically the American identity in the 1970s. Other unit activities will reinforce this concept. Teachers should revisit the identity generalizations regularly throughout the unit and make specific connections to the 1970s.

Literature Analysis Model

The Literature Analysis Model (see Figure 3) encourages students to consider seven aspects of a selection they are reading: key words, tone, mood, imagery, symbolism, key ideas, and the structure of writing (Center for Gifted Education, 2011; McKeague, 2009; National Governors Association Center for Best Practices & Council of Chief State School Officers, 2010). After reading a selection, this model helps students to organize their initial responses and provides them with a basis for discussing the piece in small or large groups. Whenever possible, students should be allowed to underline and make notes as they read the material. After marking the text, they can organize their notes into the model.

HANDOUT

Literature Analysis Model

Chosen or assigned text: _____	
Key words:	
Important ideas:	
Tone:	
Mood:	
Imagery:	
Symbolism:	
Structure of writing:	

Figure 3. Literature Analysis Model.

Suggested questions for completing and discussing the model are:

1. **Key words:** What words are important for understanding the selection? Which words did the author use for emphasis?
2. **Important ideas:** What is the main idea of the selection? What are other important ideas in the selection?
3. **Tone:** What is the attitude or what are the feelings of the author toward the subject of the selection? What words does the author use to indicate tone?
4. **Mood:** What emotions do you feel when reading the selection? How do the setting, images, objects, and details contribute to the mood?
5. **Imagery:** What are examples of the descriptive language that is used to create sensory impressions in the selection?
6. **Symbolism:** What symbols are used to represent other things?
7. **Structure of writing:** What are some important characteristics of the way this piece is written? How do the parts of this selection fit together and relate to each other? How do structural elements contribute to the meaning of the piece?

After students have completed their Literature Analysis Models individually, they should compare their answers in small groups. These small groups may compile a composite model that includes the ideas of all members. Following the small-group work, teachers have several options for using the models. For instance, they may ask each group to report to the class, they may ask groups to post their composite models, or they may develop a new Literature Analysis Model with the class based on the small-group work. It is important for teachers to hold a whole-group discussion as the final aspect of implementing this model as a teaching-learning device. Teachers are also encouraged to display the selection on a document camera or overhead projector as it is discussed and make appropriate annotations. The teacher should record ideas, underline words listed, and call attention to student responses visually. The teacher should conclude the discussion by asking open-ended follow-up questions. For more information about analyzing literature, see Center for Gifted Education (2011).

Primary Source Document Analysis Model

The Primary Source Document Analysis Model has been developed as a way to teach students:

» how to interpret a historical document,
» how to pose questions to ask about it, and
» how to examine information in the document critically.

The handout (see Figure 4) is designed to assist students as they work through this Primary Source Document Analysis Model. The information that follows includes additional questions and ideas meant to facilitate use of the model. This questions in this model assume the author had an agenda or plan about a specific issue. Thus, it may not be appropriate for use with all primary source documents. For more information about primary sources, see Center for Gifted Education (2007) and Library of Congress (n.d.).

What is the title of the document? Why was it given this title? Students should write the title of the document in this space. The discussion should include probing of why the document was given this title.

What is your reaction to the document? The student will engage with the document and use prior knowledge to make some initial observations and comments. To do that, have students read the document and answer the questions based on their first impressions. You could also revisit the questions on this part of the model after a more thorough analysis of the document has been completed.

When was the document written? Why was it written? The student will focus on the context of the document, as well as its purpose. In order to do that, students must consider the following:

1. Students need to understand the beliefs, norms, and values—the *culture*—of the period in which the document was developed.
2. Students also need to think about other *relevant events* and prevalent opinions concerning this issue that were occurring at the time the document was created.
3. Students need to consider the *context*. Additional questions to explore the context could include:
   ○ Who had control of the situation? Who wanted control, but didn't have it?

HANDOUT

Primary Source Document Analysis Model

Document: _____

What is the title of the document? Why was it given this title?

Title:
Why do you think it was given this title?
Which words in the title are especially important? Why?

What is your reaction to the document?

What is the first thing about this document that draws your attention?
What is in the document that surprises you, or that you didn't expect?
What are some of the powerful ideas expressed in the document?
What feelings does the primary source cause in you?
What questions does it raise for you?

When was the document written? Why was it written?

Who is the author(s)?
When was the document written?
What do you know about the culture of the time period in which the document was written?
What were the important events occurring at the time the document was written?
What was the author's purpose in writing this document?
Who is the intended audience?
What biases do you see in the author's text?

What are the important ideas in this document?

What problems or events does the document address?
What is the author's main point or argument?
What actions or outcomes does the author expect? From whom?
How do you think this author would define *American identity*? What elements of the American identity does the author see as being threatened or cultivated? Why?

What is your evaluation of this document?

Is this document authentic? How do you know?
Is this author a reliable source for addressing this issue/problem?
How representative is this document of the views of the people at this time in history?
How does this document compare with others of the same time period?
What could have been the possible consequences of this document?
What actually happened as a result of this document? Discuss the long-term, short-term, and unintended consequences.
What interpretation of this historical period does this document provide?
How does this document contribute to your understanding of the American identity during this time period?

Figure 4. Primary Source Document Analysis Model.

- ○ Who and what were important to people at this time?
- ○ What did people at this time hope for or value?
- ○ Was this issue a new one, an ongoing one, one that was being debated frequently at the time, or one in which few people were interested?
- ○ What were the major events occurring at the time the document was written?
- ○ What were the societal trends occurring at the time this document was written?

4. Once students have determined the context for the document, the next step is to focus on the *purpose* of the document. Additional questions to explore the purpose include:
   - ○ Why did the author write this?
   - ○ Did a specific event or opinion of the time inspire this document? If so, what was it?
   - ○ Did the author have a personal experience that led him or her to write this?
   - ○ Did someone require or ask the author to write the document?
   - ○ How does the purpose affect the content of the document?

5. Connected to purpose is the *audience*. The same author may write differently for specific groups of people. The primary audience can affect the interpretation of the document.
   - ○ For whom was the document created?
   - ○ How did the proposed audience affect the content of the document?

What are the important ideas in this document? Once students understand the context and purpose of the document, they will analyze what the document means. Additional questions for probing student understanding of the document's *important ideas* could include:

- » What assumptions/values/feelings are reflected in the document?
- » What is the author's opinion about the issue?
- » Is the author empathetic about the situation, or critical of it?
- » Is the author an insider or outsider relative to the issue? Is the author personally involved with the issue or is he or she an observer?

Finally, because the author had a purpose for writing the document, he or she must expect something to happen as a result. These questions can provide additional prompting of student understanding of the *possible results*:

- » Who does the author expect to take action in this situation?
- » Does the author expect people to change their opinions, to take a specific action, or to consider a new idea?

What is your evaluation of this document? Students will evaluate the document to identify its effectiveness, both for those in the past and for us in the present.

1. The first set of questions focuses on the *authenticity* and *reliability* of a source to help students decide whether or not a document is what it claims or appears to be.
   - ○ Authenticity relates to whether the document is real, and not altered or an imitation. Historical documents often have passed through many hands; in doing so, editors or translators may have altered the words or the meaning of the document accidentally or intentionally to reflect their own agendas (Center for Gifted Education, 2007).

○ Reliability relates to the author's qualifications for addressing a given issue or event. In order to write something reliable, authors need to have adequate information and experience with the topic being discussed (Center for Gifted Education, 2007).

Additional questions for discussing the authenticity and reliability of a source are:
○ Could the document have been fabricated, edited, or mistranslated?
○ What evidence do you need to verify the accuracy of the document?
○ What evidence do you have to show that the document was altered at a later time?
○ How reliable is this author?
○ Is the author an authority on this issue, or does he or she have sufficient knowledge to write about it?

2. The second set of questions focuses on how *representative* a document is of views of the time. This requires students to identify the prevalence of the stated ideas in society at the time the document was written.
    ○ Would many, some, or few people have agreed with the ideas stated in this document?
    ○ How do the ideas in this document relate to the context of the period in which it was written?
    ○ How does this document compare with others from the same period? Are there other documents from the time that express similar ideas? Different ideas?
    ○ What other information might you need to confirm this?

3. The third set of questions relates to considering the *consequences* of a document. First, students must consider the possible outcomes and then the actual ones. By considering the possible outcomes, students can see that multiple options for outcomes existed.
    ○ What could the possible consequences of this document have been?
    ○ What might happen if the author's plans were implemented?
    ○ What could the reaction to the author be when people read this?
    ○ How might this document affect or change public opinions?
    ○ What actually happened as a result of this document?
    ○ How did this document affect people's lives or events at the time (short-term effects)?
    ○ How did the document affect people at other times in the past, or how does it affect us today (long-term effects)?
    ○ What were the unintended consequences of this document?

4. The fourth set of questions helps students to determine *how the interpretation informs the reader* about the historical period:
    ○ What new interpretation of the historical period does this document provide for the reader?
    ○ How does the document provide an interpretation about the historical period that is not provided through other materials of the time?
    ○ How does this interpretation inform us about the American identity during this time period?

The implementation of this model may be handled similarly to the way in which discussions are held using the Literature Analysis Model: After students have completed their Primary Source Document Analysis Models individually, they should compare their answers in small groups. These small groups may compile a composite model that includes the ideas of all members. Following the small-group work, teachers have several options for using the models, including developing a composite, whole-class model, or posting group models and discussing them. It is important for teachers to hold a group discussion as the final aspect of implementing this model as a teaching-learning device. Teachers are also encouraged to display the selection on a document camera or overhead projector as it is discussed and make appropriate annotations. The teacher should record ideas, underline words listed, and call attention to student responses visually. The teacher should conclude the discussion by asking open-ended follow-up questions.

Music Analysis Model

The Music Analysis Model (see Figure 5) has been developed as a means for teaching students:
  » how to interpret lyrics from a song,
  » how to pose questions to ask about it, and
  » how to examine information in the song critically.

When working with specific songs, encourage students to think critically about both the *lyrics* and *orchestration*, keeping the elements of identity in mind. The Music Analysis Model uses the same key questions as the Primary Source Document Analysis Model, but with wording specifically related to songs:
  » What is the title of the song? Why was it given this title?
  » What is your reaction to the song?
  » When was the song written? Why was it written?
  » What are the important ideas in this song?
  » What is your evaluation of this song?

As such, many of the same questions listed above for the Primary Source Document Analysis Model may be used for additional probing into student understanding. For additional suggestions about the implementation of this model, please see the note regarding how to manage class discussions after students have completed the Primary Source Document Analysis Model.

Art Analysis Model

The Art Analysis Model (see Figure 6) has been developed as a means for teaching students:
  » how to interpret a piece of artwork,
  » how to pose questions to ask about it, and
  » how to examine the piece of artwork critically.

When working with specific pieces of art, encourage students to think critically about both the *image* and the *materials*, keeping the elements of identity in mind. The Art Analysis Model

---

HANDOUT

Music Analysis Model

Song Title:_____

What is the title of the song? Why was it given this title?

Title:
Why do you think it was given this title?
Which words in the title are especially important? Why?

What is your reaction to the song?

What is the first thing about this song that draws your attention?
What is in the song that surprises you, or that you didn't expect?
What are some of the powerful ideas expressed in the song?
What feelings does the song cause in you?
What questions does it raise for you?

When was the song written? Why was it written?

Who is the songwriter(s)?
When was the song written?
What is the song's purpose? To entertain? To dance to? To critique something?
What were the important events occurring at the time the song was written?
Who is the intended audience?
What biases do you see in the author's lyrics?

What are the important ideas in this song?

Lyrics	Music/Accompaniment
What is the subject of the song? Summarize the song.	Describe the music or melody of this song. Is it fast-paced or slow? Does it have low notes or high notes? Is it melodic or does it have lots of percussion?
What are the main points of the song? What is the song saying about the subject?	What feelings do you get from the music? Why?
What mood/values/feelings does the singer have about the topic?	How does the tone or mood of the music fit with the lyrics? Why might this be?

What is your evaluation of this song?

What new or different interpretation of this historical period does this song provide?
What does this song portray about American identity or how Americans felt at the time?

Figure 5. Music Analysis Model.

HANDOUT

Art Analysis Model

Artist: _____

Artwork/Image: _____

What is the title of the artwork? Why was it given this title?

Title:
Why do you think it was given this title?
Which words in the title are especially important? Why?
What does the title reveal about the artwork?

What do you see in the artwork?

What objects, shapes, or people do you see?
What colors does the artist use? Why?
Are the images in the work realistic or abstract?
What materials does the artist use? Why?

What is your reaction to the image?

What is the first thing about this image that draws your attention?
What is in the image that surprises you, or that you didn't expect?
What are some of the powerful ideas expressed in the image?
What feelings does the image cause in you?
What questions does it raise for you?

When was the image produced? Why was it produced?

Who is the artist?
When was the artwork produced?
What were the important events occurring at the time the artwork was produced?
What was the author's purpose in producing this artwork?
Who is the intended audience?

What are the important ideas in this artwork?

What assumptions/values/feelings are reflected in the artwork?
What are the artist's views about the issue(s)?

What is your evaluation of this artwork?

What new or different interpretation of this historical period does this artwork provide?
What does this artwork portray about American identity or how Americans felt at the time?

Figure 6. Art Analysis Model.

uses many of the same key questions as the Primary Source Document Analysis Model, but with wording specifically related to artwork:

» What is the title of the artwork? Why was it given this title?
» What do you see in the artwork?
» What is your reaction to the image?
» When was the image produced? Why was it produced?
» What are the important ideas in this artwork?
» What is your evaluation of this artwork?

For additional suggestions about the implementation of this model, please see the note regarding how to manage class discussions after students have completed the Primary Source Document Analysis Model.

Summary: Teaching Models

The five teaching models that are included in this unit are essential for facilitating discussions and attaining unit objectives. Teachers should familiarize themselves with these models before beginning the unit and attempt to use them with fidelity. It is important that they use the models repeatedly, as students need practice interacting with the models' components and understanding the questions.

LESSON 1

"It Seems the Good Die Young": The 70s Begin

Alignment of Unit Goals

» Goal 1: To understand the concept of identity in 1970s America.
» Goal 2: To develop skills in historical analysis and song and artwork interpretation.
» Goal 3: To develop analytical and interpretive skills in literature.
» Goal 4: To develop an understanding of historical events occurring in the United States during the 1970s.

Unit Objectives

» To describe how the American identity changed during the 1970s.
» To describe how changes in American identity in the 1970s were revealed in the music, art, and literature of the decade.

» To define the context in which a song or piece of art was produced and the implications of context for understanding the artifact.

» To describe a writer's or artist's intent in producing a given song or piece of art based on understanding of text and context.

» To describe what a selected literary passage means.

» To describe major historical events during the 1970s that affected the American identity.

» To describe music, art, and literature of the 1970s that reflected the American identity.

Resources for Unit Implementation

» **Handout 1.1:** *Breakfast of Champions* Q & A

» **Handout 1.2:** Music Analysis Model

» **Handout 1.3:** Music of the Early 1970s

» **Handout 1.4:** Identity Chart

» **Handout 1.5:** Identity Generalizations

» **Handout 1.6:** Pet Rocks Unit Project

» **Read:** The opening pages (up to p. 20) of *Breakfast of Champions* by Kurt Vonnegut (1973/1999). An online excerpt is available at http://www.ereader.com/servlet/mw?t= book_excerpt&bookid=6542&si=59.

» **Listen:** "Abraham, Martin, and John" (Holler, 1968) by Dion. The song is available on You-Tube.

» **Listen:** "Piano Man" by Billy Joel (1973); "Inner City Blues (Make Me Wanna Holler)" (Gaye & Nyx, 1971) by Marvin Gaye; "Born to Run" by Bruce Springsteen (1975); "I'm a Worried Man" (Cash & Cash, 1974) by Johnny Cash; and "What's Going On" by Marvin Gaye (1971). All songs are available on YouTube.

» **Listen:** "Let It Be" by The Beatles (McCartney, 1970), "Bridge Over Troubled Water" by Simon & Garfunkel (Simon, 1970), ""I'll Be There" by The Jackson 5 (Gordy, West, Davis, & Hutch, 1970), "Raindrops Keep Falling on My Head" (David & Bacharach, 1969) by B. J. Thomas. All songs are available on YouTube.

Key Terms

» *Assassination:* the murder of a political figure, often by a surprise attack

» *Recession:* a time of reduced economic activity, varying in scope and duration

Learning Experiences

1. Explain to students that during the 1970s, the United States went through economic, international, and cultural changes that affected Americans' perceptions of themselves, of the country, and of their role in the world. In order to understand how the events of this decade shaped the views of the average American, students are going to examine the music, literature, and art that was produced and consumed in the U.S. at the time.

2. Tell students that one of the popular authors of the 1970s was Kurt Vonnegut (1973/1999). Have students read the opening pages of his novel *Breakfast of Champions*. Have them

complete Handout 1.1 (*Breakfast of Champions* Q & A). **Ask:** What is your reaction to this excerpt? Why? What type of lives do the characters seem to lead? How do these characters feel about their country? What criticisms do they make of their country? Why? What do they seem to be searching for? To understand these attitudes, let's review what's went on during the time the book was written.

3. **Ask:** What events do you remember from 1968? (e.g., assassinations of Dr. Martin Luther King, Jr. and Robert F. Kennedy, Tet Offensive in Vietnam, violent clash at the Democratic National Convention, etc.) Give students a copy of Handout 1.2 (Music Analysis Model). Play Dion's song "Abraham, Martin, and John" (Holler, 1968). Together, complete the analysis of the song. **Ask:** Based on this song, what was the mood of the U.S. at the end of 1968?

4. Explain to students that 1969 seemed to restore some hope in the American people as Neil Armstrong walked on the moon and the Woodstock music and art festival took place without violence. But, as the 1960s ended and the 1970s began, events took place that affected the American people. Using your textbook, review with students President Nixon's plan for Vietnamization and the invasion of Cambodia, the protest and violence at Kent State University that resulted, the recession of 1970, the Watergate crisis, and the 1973 Yom Kippur War, which led to the Organization of the Petroleum Exporting Countries (OPEC) putting an embargo on oil to the U.S. **Ask:** What do you think the effect of these events were on people in the U.S.? Why? How might these events explain the attitudes in the Vonnegut reading you started with at the beginning of the lesson?

5. Tell students that to try to understand how the ordinary American felt, they will look at some of the songs being produced during this time. Put students in groups of five, give each student Handout 1.3 (Music of the Early 1970s) and one of the following songs to analyze: "Piano Man" by Billy Joel (1973); "Inner City Blues" (Gaye & Nyx, 1971) by Marvin Gaye; "Born to Run" by Bruce Springsteen (1975); "I'm a Worried Man" (Cash & Cash, 1974) by Johnny Cash; and "What's Goin' On?" by Marvin Gaye (1971). Have students analyze their assigned song and lyrics.

6. Then, have students in their group share their findings and complete Handout 1.3 together. Provide students with access to the lyrics of the following songs while in their groups: "Let It Be" (McCartney, 1970) by The Beatles; "Bridge Over Troubled Water" (Simon, 1970) by Simon & Garfunkel; "I'll Be There" (Gordy, West, Davis, & Hutch, 1970) by The Jackson 5; and "Raindrops Keep Falling on My Head" (David & Bacharach, 1969) by B. J. Thomas. The lyrics to each song can be found through a Google search. Discuss student responses.

7. Tell students that as they study the 1970s, they will focus on American identity and how it changed throughout the last half of the 20th century and how those changes were revealed in the music, art, and literature of the time. In a whole group, brainstorm together responses to the following and put student responses on the board to examine. **Ask:** What is identity? What are the various aspects or parts of someone's identity? Why is a person's identity important? What role does a person's identity play in how he or she acts or what he or she does? Discuss student responses as a class. (*Note:* If you have previously done this activity in a previous unit, you can skip this step.)

8. Distribute Handout 1.4 (Identity Chart) to students and explain that some scholars have developed categories of elements that define identity such as family, race, ethnicity, indi-

viduality, beliefs, values, nationality, social class, and time and place. They will use these to try to define American identity in the 1970s As a whole group, work through the pieces of the wheel this first time. **Ask:**

a. Time and place: What was our nationality? What were our national symbols and sources of pride? What shared symbols or traditions represent American identity and are seen as meaningful by most Americans?

b. History and myths: What was the shared background or heritage of the U.S.? What recent events or experiences shaped American views?

c. Culture and traditions: What were American values in the 1970s?

d. Race and ethnicity: What was the status of the races in the 1970s? What was the role of ethnicity in the 1970s?

e. Civic identity: What was the role of the citizen in America? What were our rights and duties as citizens?

f. International role: What beliefs did America have about itself and others in the world?

g. Economy: What does the U.S. produce? How did the U.S. generate revenue? What types of jobs did most people have? What was the status of the U.S. economy?

9. Explain to students that they will look at how the events and experiences of the 1970s altered American identity using a set of generalizations. Distribute Handout 1.5 (Identity Generalizations) to students and explain that they will work through it together using Handout 1.2.

a. The first generalization is *"Identity changes with new ideas, experiences, conditions, or in response to other expressions of identity."* **Ask:** What new ideas, experiences or conditions arose during the 1960s? Have students hypothesize about how these affected American identity.

b. The second generalization is *"Identity is created by a group, person, or outsiders, and self-created identities may be different from how others see one's self."* **Ask:** How did America see itself in the world? How did the Soviet Union see America? Vietnam? China? How did these different views shape America's role in the world?

c. The third generalization is *"There are multiple elements of identity and at different times, different elements have greater or lesser importance."* **Ask:** Which elements of identity were most significant in 1973?

d. The fourth generalization is *"Although members of a group or society may have different individual identities, they still share particular elements of identity."* **Ask:** Despite individual differences, which elements of identity did all Americans have in common?

10. Explain to students that they will use these generalizations on identity and the concept of identity as they study the events of the late 20th century and examine the effect of those events on American identity.

11. Tell students that this unit will cover many different things, and they will do a project about what they think were the most influential people and events of the 1970s. Assign students Handout 1.6 (Pet Rocks Unit Project) to be due at the end of the unit.

Assessing Student Learning

»   Handout 1.1 (*Breakfast of Champions* Q & A)
»   Handout 1.2 (Music Analysis Model)
»   Handout 1.3 (Music of the Early 1970s)
»   Handout 1.4 (Identity Chart)
»   Handout 1.5 (Identity Generalizations)
»   Discussions

Extending Student Learning

The following are optional activities for extending student learning in this lesson:

»   As an independent or group research activity, have students research various aspects of popular culture in the 1970s and share their findings with their classmates in an interactive format. Possible topics could include fashions, fads, social movements, sports personalities, and art, music, and literature movements.
»   President Nixon visited China in 1972. Have students locate photographs and other resources to provide an overview of this event. Students should develop a final product that reflects the importance of his visit.
»   Have students conduct additional research about Kurt Vonnegut's life and works. Have them present their findings using digital technology.

Name: _____ Date: _____

HANDOUT 1.1
Breakfast of Champions Q & A

Directions: After reading the beginning of *Breakfast of Champions,* complete the following questions.

1. What is your reaction to this excerpt? Why?

    _____

    _____

    _____

2. What type of lives do the characters seem to lead?

    _____

    _____

    _____

3. How do these characters feel about their country?

    _____

    _____

    _____

4. What criticisms do they make of their country? Why?

    _____

    _____

    _____

5. What do they seem to be searching for?

    _____

    _____

    _____

6. List all of the events you can remember from 1965–1969. How might these events explain the feelings in this excerpt?

    _____

    _____

    _____

Name:_____ Date:_____

HANDOUT 1.2
Music Analysis Model

Directions: After listening to "Abraham, Martin, and John," please complete the following questions.

Song Title:_____

What is the title of the song? Why was it given this title?

Title:
Why do you think it was given this title?
Which words in the title are especially important? Why?

What is your reaction to the song?

What is the first thing about this song that draws your attention?
What is in the song that surprises you, or that you didn't expect?
What are some of the powerful ideas expressed in the song?
What feelings does the song cause in you?
What questions does it raise for you?

Name: _____ Date: _____

When was the song written? Why was it written?

Who is the songwriter(s)?
When was the song written?
What is the song's purpose? To entertain? To dance to? To critique something?
What were the important events occurring at the time the song was written?
Who is the intended audience?
What biases do you see in the author's lyrics?

What are the important ideas in this song?

Lyrics	Music/Accompaniment
What is the subject of the song? Summarize the song.	Describe the music or melody of this song. Is it fast-paced or slow? Does it have low notes or high notes? Is it melodic or does it have lots of percussion?
What are the main points of the song? What is the song saying about the subject?	What feelings do you get from the music? Why?
What mood/values/feelings does the singer have about the topic?	How does the tone or mood of the music fit with the lyrics? Why might this be?

What is your evaluation of this song?

What new or different interpretation of this historical period does this song provide?
What does this song portray about American identity or how Americans felt at the time?

Name:_____ Date:_____

HANDOUT 1.3
Music of the Early 1970s

Directions: After analyzing your assigned song, complete the chart and the questions based on the class discussion of the music.

	"Piano Man" by Billy Joel	"Inner City Blues" by Marvin Gaye	"I'm a Worried Man" by Johnny Cash	"Born to Run" by Bruce Springsteen	"What's Goin' On?" by Marvin Gaye
What is the topic of the song?					
What issue or concern does the song describe?					
What images and experiences does the song emphasize?					
What is the mood of the song?					

1. How are these songs similar?

    _____

    _____

2. How are they different?

    _____

    _____

3. In 1970, four of the top 10 songs of the year were "Let It Be" by the Beatles, "Bridge Over Troubled Water" by Simon and Garfunkel, "I'll Be There" by The Jackson 5, and "Raindrops Keep Fallin' on My Head" by B. J. Thomas.
    ○   What are the messages of these songs?
    ○   What are the songs' moods?

    _____

    _____

4. What do the popularity of the songs you analyzed and the list of the top songs of 1970 tell us about the American societal mindset of the early 1970s? What can you infer about how people felt about their lives and the state of society?

    _____

    _____

HANDOUT 1.4

Identity Chart

Directions: Complete each box with the elements that define each category of identity.

Identity	
	Time and Place
	Culture and Traditions
	History and Myths
	International Role
	Economy
	Civic Identity
	Race/Ethnicity

Name:_____ Date:_____

HANDOUT 1.5

Identity Generalizations

Directions: Use these generalizations to frame your discussion of how the events and experiences of the 1970s altered the American identity.

Identity changes with new ideas, experiences, conditions, or in response to other expressions of identity.
Identity is created by a group, person, or outsiders, and self-created identities may be different from how others see one's self.
There are multiple elements of identity and at different times, different elements have greater or lesser importance.
Although members of a group or society may have different individual identities, they still share particular elements of identity.

HANDOUT 1.6

Pet Rocks Unit Project

One of the popular fads of the 1970s was the Pet Rock. Pet Rocks were collectibles invented by advertising executive Gary Dahl.

Your task: Based on your understanding of the 1970s, create a set of Pet Rocks that depict influential figures or events that shaped American identity or values in the 1970s. (*Note:* You may want to research Pet Rocks beforehand to get an idea of what they looked like.) The assignment is due at the end of the unit. Follow the instructions below to complete your Pet Rocks.

1. You need to research and choose 8–10 people or events that will appear on your rocks.

2. Find enough rocks so that you have one for each person or event.

3. Write a justification for including these people or events that explains their significance in American culture and their importance to American identity in the 1970s.

4. You may include any figures from the decade, and you are not restricted to the ones you listened to or read about in the unit. You may expand your research to include authors, music groups, sports figures, political figures, actors, or any other significant individuals from the 1970s.

5. You may paint or color your rocks and attach decorations to the rock surface.

LESSON 2

Women's Liberation

Alignment of Unit Goals

- » Goal 1: To understand the concept of identity in 1970s America.
- » Goal 2: To develop skills in historical analysis and song and artwork interpretation.
- » Goal 3: To develop analytical and interpretive skills in literature.
- » Goal 4: To develop an understanding of historical events occurring in the United States during the 1970s.

Unit Objectives

- » To describe how the American identity changed during the 1970s.
- » To describe how changes in American identity in the 1970s were revealed in the music, art, and literature of the decade.
- » To define the context in which a song or piece of art was produced and the implications of context for understanding the artifact.
- » To describe a writer's or artist's intent in producing a given song or piece of art based on understanding of text and context.
- » To describe what a selected literary passage means.

» To describe major historical events during the 1970s that affected the American identity.
» To describe music, art, and literature of the 1970s that reflected the American identity.

Resources for Unit Implementation

» **Handout 2.1:** The Women's Liberation Movement Q & A
» **Handout 2.2:** *The Power of the Positive Woman* Q & A
» **Handout 2.3:** Portrayal of Women in 1970s Music
» **Handout 2.4:** The Identity of Women
» **Handout 2.5:** Groups Fighting for Civil Rights in the 1970s
» **Listen:** "I Am Woman" (Reddy & Burton, 1971) by Helen Reddy. The song is available on YouTube.
» **Read:** "I Want a Wife" by Judy Brady (1971). An online version is available at http://www.columbia.edu/~sss31/rainbow/wife.html
» **Read:** "The Housewife's Moment of Truth" by Jane O'Reilly (1971), available at http://nymag.com/news/features/46167/
» **Read:** "What Would It Be Like If Women Win" by Gloria Steinem (1970), available at http://jackiewhiting.net/ap/Steinem.htm
» **Read:** Text from the Equal Rights Amendment (ERA), available at http://www.equalrightsamendment.org/
» **Read:** An excerpt from *The Power of the Positive Woman* by Phyllis Schlafly (1977). An online excerpt is available at http://jackiewhiting.net/Women/Power/Schlafly.htm.
» **Listen:** "(You Make Me Feel Like) A Natural Woman" (Goffin, King, & Wexler, 1967) by Carole King; "Me and Bobby McGee" (Kristofferson & Foster, 1969) by Janis Joplin; "Reach Out and Touch (Somebody's Hand)" (Ashford & Simpson, 1970) by Diana Ross; "I Will Survive" (Perren & Fekaris, 1978) by Gloria Gaynor; and "Queens of Noise" (Bizeau, 1977) by The Runaways.

Key Terms

» *Civil rights:* rights that protect one's individual freedoms within a society
» *Liberation:* the seeking of equal status or just treatment for a group believed to be discriminated against
» *Movement:* a series of organized activities to obtain an objective
» *Suffrage:* the right to vote

Learning Experiences

(*Note:* Discussion of any topic related to the civil rights of a given group can elicit emotional responses. Teachers should closely monitor the class discussion, especially regarding the derogatory language used to describe different groups of people during this time period.)

1. Play Helen Reddy's song "I Am Woman" (Reddy & Burton, 1971). **Ask:** What does this song imply was the role or status of women before the 1970s? What changes is the song sug-

gesting take place in the role or status of women in the 1970s? Explain that students will be looking at the Women's Liberation Movement of the 1970s.

2. Tell students they have studied women's rights movements at different times in history. **Ask:** Who are some women's rights leaders you remember and what were they demanding? What was the state of the women's rights movement in the 1960s? Explain to students that in 1967, the National Organization for Women (NOW) was formed. NOW was pushing for the passage of the Equal Rights Amendment (ERA), which would provide full equality under the law for women. To achieve this, NOW led a "Strike for Equality" parade in New York City in August of 1970 and published magazines and articles to promote their views. In this lesson, they will read several articles from the early issues of *Ms.* magazine.

3. Break students into groups of three. Have each member of the group read one of the following: "I Want a Wife" by Judy Brady (1971), "The Housewife's Moment of Truth" by Jane O'Reilly (1971), or "What Would It Be Like If Women Win" by Gloria Steinem (1970). The URLs for each essay are listed under "Resources for Unit Implementation." Have students answer the questions on Handout 2.1 (The Women's Liberation Movement Q & A), then share their reading with the group. **Ask:** How are the arguments of these three women similar? In goals, in concerns, in tone? How do the ideas of these three women differ? Why might that be? What can you conclude or summarize about the Women's Liberation Movement from these three documents and their similarities and differences? How do you think Americans responded to these ideas? Why?

4. Show students the text of the ERA from http://www.equalrightsamendment.org. **Ask:** What does the ERA say? How does this fit with the ideas of the women you read? Tell students that the ERA passed Congress in 1972 and then went to the states to be ratified. Thirty-eight of the 50 states had to ratify the ERA to add it to the Constitution. **Ask:** What might the effects of passing the ERA passing have been for the U.S.? Tell students that in 1973, the Supreme Court passed the *Roe v. Wade* decision, which said women's right to privacy under the 14th Amendment applied to abortions, and that states could not restrict women's ability to get an abortion during her first trimester. Many people also saw this as a gain for women's rights.

5. Tell students that during this time, efforts to stop the ratification of the ERA began. **Ask:** Why might this be? One of the voices of the STOP-ERA movement was Phyllis Schlafly. Have students read *The Power of the Positive Woman* by Phyllis Schlafly (1977) and answer the questions on Handout 2.2 (*The Power of the Positive Woman* Q & A). **Ask:** Does it surprise you that a woman was opposing the ERA? Why or why not? What does Mrs. Schlafly's article reveal about the women's liberation movement at the time? Why was there such a wide range of opinions about the status of women?

6. Tell students that to see the more day-to-day views of women, they will look at popular songs by female artists of the early 1970s. Listen to and read the lyrics of the following songs as a class (lyrics can be found through a Google search). As they listen, have students jot down what roles/behaviors/traits they see in women in each song using Handout 2.3 (Portrayal of Women in 1970s Music). Listen to "(You Make Me Feel Like) A Natural Woman" (Gofflin, King, & Wexler, 1967) by Carole King; "Me and Bobby McGee" (Kristofferson & Foster, 1969) by Janis Joplin; "Reach Out and Touch (Somebody's Hand)" (Ashford & Simpson, 1970) by Diana Ross; "I Will Survive" (Perren & Fekaris, 1978) by Gloria

Gaynor; and "Queens of Noise" (Bizeau, 1977) by The Runaways. **Ask:** How do the images of women in these songs fit with the ideas of the Women's Liberation Movement (i.e., the ideas expressed in the essays of Steinem, O'Reilly, Brady)? How do the images of women in these songs fit the more traditional view of women (i.e., Schlafly's view)? What do these songs reveal about what the average American's view on women's liberation was? How widespread do you think the ideas of Gloria Steinem and women's liberation were? How widespread do you think the ideas of Phyllis Schlafly were? What can you tell about American beliefs regarding gender roles from these different readings and songs? Tell students that by the deadline in 1982, the ERA had only been passed by 35 states and was never ratified.

7. Have students complete Handout 2.4 (The Identity of Women) in small groups and then discuss as a whole class. **Ask:** What do you think most Americans felt about the status of women in society?

8. Distribute Handout 2.5 (Groups Fighting for Civil Rights in the 1970s). Tell students that they will revisit this chart throughout the unit as they discuss various groups fighting for their civil rights during the 1970s. Have them complete the row for "women," describing the rights desired, the major individuals involved, key events, and outcomes.

Assessing Student Learning

» Handout 2.1 (The Women's Liberation Movement Q & A)
» Handout 2.2 (*The Power of the Positive Woman* Q & A)
» Handout 2.3 (Portrayal of Women in 1970s Music)
» Handout 2.4 (The Identity of Women)
» Handout 2.5 (Groups Fighting for Civil Rights in the 1970s)
» Discussions

Extending Student Learning

The following are other optional activities for extending student learning in this lesson:

» Have students create a mosaic of historical photographs that depict different aspects of the fight for women's rights. When students present their mosaics, they should provide commentary about each photograph.

» Have students write and present their own poems about strong women who have played an important role in their lives.

» Have students use video footage to create a collage of images that reveal how women have been portrayed in film and television either before the 1970s or since the Women's Liberation Movement. Students should include music and a voiceover narrating the collage.

» Have students research and report about how men's lives were changed by the women's movement.

HANDOUT 2.1

The Women's Liberation Movement Q & A

Directions: Answer the questions for your reading only. Be prepared to tell your group about your reading.

"I Want a Wife" by Judy Brady

1. What roles does Brady say a wife has?

   _____

   _____

2. What does she suggest about men when she says they expect certain things done by a woman? What statement is she making about men in general—about their attitudes and behaviors?

   _____

   _____

3. What does she imply is happening to women in their current status?

   _____

   _____

4. What is the tone or mood of this piece?

   _____

   _____

5. What is her point in saying she wants a wife? How is this a women's rights argument?

   _____

   _____

"The Housewife's Moment of Truth" by Jane O'Reilly

1. What is happening in all of the situations when O'Reilly says "click"? What is "clicking"? For whom?

   _____

   _____

2. What roles does O'Reilly say women currently fill?

   _____

   _____

Handout 2.1: The Women's Liberation Movement Q & A, continued
_____

3. Why isn't women's liberation just about equal pay for equal work for her? What does she want?

    _____

    _____

4. Why does she view men as an obstacle to achieving her goals?

    _____

    _____

5. What rules does she devise for women? How will these rules address the grievances she has?

    _____

    _____

"What Would It Be Like if Women Win" by Gloria Steinem

1. What is the tone or mood of this piece?

    _____

    _____

2. What changes in society does Steinem ask for? What does her "Women's Lib Utopia" look like?

    _____

    _____

3. What obstacles does she feel there are to achieving this?

    _____

    _____

4. What benefits does she feel her Utopia brings to women? Men? The family?

    _____

    _____

5. Why does she present her argument in this way? Why portray her Utopia this way?

    _____

    _____

Summary:

1. Are all three of these women seeking the same thing?

    _____

    _____

Handout 2.1: The Women's Liberation Movement Q & A, continued
_____

2. How are the arguments of these three women similar? In goals, in concerns, in tone?

   _____

   _____

3. How do the ideas of these three women differ? Why might that be?

   _____

   _____

4. What can we conclude or summarize about the Women's Liberation Movement from these three documents and their similarities and differences?

   _____

   _____

5. Which woman's argument is the most convincing? Why?

   _____

   _____

6. How do you think Americans responded to these ideas? Why?

   _____

   _____

Name: _____ Date: _____

HANDOUT 2.2

The Power of the Positive Woman Q & A

Directions: Answer these questions after reading *The Power of the Positive Woman* by Phyllis Schlafly.

1. Why does Schlafly call the Women's Liberation Movement a "dead-end road"? Why is it heading in the wrong direction?

   _____

   _____

   _____

2. Schlafly portrays women's liberationists as negative and pessimistic and her own view as positive. What does she mean when she calls their views negative? Why is her approach more positive in her mind? How would the women you read before this respond to these labels and this argument?

   _____

   _____

   _____

3. What differences between men and women does Schlafly list? Why does she feel these differences are good and not negative things?

   _____

   _____

   _____

4. How does she view the maternal and housewife roles of women? Why?

   _____

   _____

   _____

5. How would the other three women respond to this article? Why?

   _____

   _____

   _____

HANDOUT 2.3

Portrayal of Women in 1970s Music

Directions: Complete this chart with your group members after you have read the lyrics and listened to songs by popular female artists of the early 1970s.

	Role of Women	Behaviors of Women	Traits of Women
"(You Make Me Feel Like) A Natural Woman" by Carole King			
"Me and Bobby McGee" by Janis Joplin			
"Reach Out and Touch (Somebody's Hand)" by Diana Ross			
"I Will Survive" by Gloria Gaynor			
"Queens of Noise" by The Runaways			

HANDOUT 2.4
The Identity of Women

Directions: Complete this chart with your group members. Be prepared to share your responses during the whole-class discussion.

There are multiple elements of identity and at different times, different elements have greater or lesser importance.
Which elements of identity was the Women's Liberation Movement arguing should be more important? What activities did women feel they should invest more time and energy into? Which aspects of the female identity did they believe should decrease in importance? Why?   How did Phyllis Schlafly respond? Which elements of female identity did she feel were more important and why?
Identity changes with new ideas, experiences, conditions, or in response to other expressions of identity.
What new conditions and circumstances were women being faced with during the 1970s? How did larger economic and social trends affect gender roles?   How did the gender role changes proposed by the Women's Liberation Movement change American identity as a whole?   Why were the changes in gender roles proposed by the Women's Liberation Movement so difficult for many to accept?

Handout 2.4: The Identity of Women, continued _____

Although members of a group or society may have different individual identities, they still share particular elements of identity.
Which elements of identity did both the women's liberation advocates and the STOP-ERA movement share? Where did they divide?
What did the different ideas about gender roles among women reveal about the United States in the 1970s?

HANDOUT 2.5
Groups Fighting for
Civil Rights in the 1970s

Directions: Complete this chart as you study various groups fighting for civil rights in the United States during the 1970s.

	Rights Desired	Major Individuals Involved	Key Events	Outcomes
Women				
Hispanics				
American Indians				
African Americans				

LESSON 3

De Colores: The Chicano Movement

Alignment of Unit Goals

» Goal 1: To understand the concept of identity in 1970s America.
» Goal 2: To develop skills in historical analysis and song and artwork interpretation.
» Goal 3: To develop analytical and interpretive skills in literature.
» Goal 4: To develop an understanding of historical events occurring in the United States during the 1970s.

Unit Objectives

» To describe how the American identity changed during the 1970s.
» To describe how changes in American identity in the 1970s were revealed in the music, art, and literature of the decade.

> » To define the context in which a song or piece of art was produced and the implications of context for understanding the artifact.
> » To describe a writer's or artist's intent in producing a given song or piece of art based on understanding of text and context.
> » To analyze the effects of given documents or artifacts on the interpretation of historical events.
> » To describe what a selected literary passage means.
> » To make inferences based on information in given passages.
> » To describe major historical events during the 1970s that affected the American identity.
> » To describe music, art, and literature of the 1970s that reflected the American identity.

Resources for Unit Implementation

> » **Handout 3.1:** De Colores
> » **Handout 3.2:** Analyzing Music of the Chicano Movement. The songs mentioned in this handout can be found at http://www.folkways.si.edu/rolas-de-aztlan-songs-of-the-chicano-movement/american-folk-latin/music/album/smithsonian.
> » **Handout 2.5:** Groups Fighting for Civil Rights in the 1970s
> » **Read:** I Am Joaquin by Rodolfo "Corky" Gonzales (1972), available at http://www.latinamericanstudies.org/latinos/joaquin.htm.
> » **View:** Murals in San Diego Chicano Park and Seattle. The murals from each can be seen at http://www.chicanoparksandiego.com/murals/index.html and http://depts.washington.edu/civilr/mecha_photos.htm.

Key Terms

> » *Chicano:* initially used as a derogatory term for Mexicans who were born in America and was perceived to be a negative ethnic stereotype. The Chicano Movement used it in a way to show unity among Mexican Americans and pride in their culture.
> » *Descent:* derivation from an ancestor; lineage
> » *Discrimination:* treatment of, or making a distinction in favor of or against, a person based on the group to which the person belongs, rather than on individual merit
> » *Mural:* a large picture painted directly on a wall or ceiling

Learning Experiences

1. Explain to students that although they focused on the African American Civil Rights Movement of the 1960s, there were other groups also pushing for greater rights at the same time. People of Hispanic descent had also been facing discrimination in the United States. During the Great Depression, noncitizens were deported; during World War II, businesses refused to hire or serve people of Hispanic descent even if they were citizens; and young Hispanic men were beaten in the 1943 Zoot Suit Riots in Los Angeles. After World War II and in the 1960s, Cesar Chavez had worked to unite farm workers to fight

for higher wages and better conditions, many of whom were of Hispanic descent. By the 1970s, the movement for rights had moved beyond working conditions and wages.

2. Give students a copy of the epic poem *I Am Joaquin* by Rodolfo "Corky" Gonzales (1972) and Handout 3.1 (De Colores). Have students read and analyze the poem individually or in small groups. Then, discuss student responses as a class. **Ask:** What does Gonzales mean when he says he is "lost in a world of confusion"? What causes this feeling for him? Why does he go through this list of historical events? Which events does he include? Why these? What point is he making? What is his message by the end of the poem? Tell students to set aside Handout 3.1 and that they will come back to it later.

3. Give students Handout 3.2 (Analyzing Music of the Chicano Movement) and have them listen to and analyze the songs in the handout individually. You can discuss each song as you go, or discuss student responses all at the end. The songs are all available at http://www.folkways.si.edu/rolas-de-aztlan-songs-of-the-chicano-movement/american-folk-latin/music/album/smithsonian. The liner notes with the lyrics are a free download at the site. **Ask:** What do you notice about the music and the sound of these songs? How does the sound of these songs compare to other music you have listened to from the 1970s? How does the mood and message of these songs compare to the mood and message of the epic poem *I Am Joaquin*? Which elements of identity are these songs stressing and finding important? What culture and traditions are they promoting? How do they view ethnicity and ethnic relations in the United States? What do they want to see happen?

4. Tell students that the last song mentions Chicano Park in San Diego and its murals. Explain that one part of the Chicano Movement was artistic expression on the sides of buildings and large walls. Have students go back to Handout 3.1 and analyze at least two murals from the San Diego Chicano Park site or from the Seattle area. Students can analyze one from each website and talk about similarities and differences between the two geographic areas of the United States. Have students complete the rest of Handout 3.1 individually or in small groups. Discuss student responses as a whole class. **Ask:** What are the major themes and topics of the murals? What was the purpose of these murals? Why were they put in such public locations outside, where they can be worn away by sun and weather? How do the topics and messages of the murals fit with the ideas in the songs you listened to? Based on the poem, songs, and murals, how would you summarize the goal and message of the Chicano Movement in the United States in the 1970s?

5. Have students take out their copies of Handout 2.5 (Groups Fighting for Civil Rights in the 1970s). Together, discuss responses to put in the column for the Chicano Movement. Have students save this chart; they will add to it as they go through the next several lessons.

Assessing Student Learning

» Handout 3.1 (De Colores)
» Handout 3.2 (Analyzing Music of the Chicano Movement)
» Handout 2.5 (Groups Fighting for Civil Rights in the 1970s)
» Discussions

Extending Student Learning

The following are optional activities for extending student learning in this lesson:

» Students may investigate the essential elements of the Chicano culture and present their findings to classmates in order to enhance background knowledge.

» Have students research Daniel DeSiga and his murals. Students should share biographical information about the artist and examples of his works. The commentary should include references to the importance of his work in the Chicano Movement.

» Have students research the iconography of works of the Chicano Movement. Have them present examples of the icons and descriptions of their importance in the Hispanic culture.

» Have students obtain a copy of the list of demands made by Chicano students during the East Los Angeles walkouts of March 1, 1968. The demands can be found at http://www.kcet.org/socal/departures/columns/Frivolous%20to%20Fundamental%20Demands%20Made%20by%20East%20Side%20High%20School%20Students.pdf. Have them respond to these questions:

  ○ What ideas and concerns do you see in the list of demands?

  ○ What surprises you about the demands?

  ○ How did the list reflect a sense of emerging political and cultural change?

HANDOUT 3.1

De Colores

Part I

Directions: Read and analyze the poem *I Am Joaquin*.

1. What does the poet mean when he says he is "lost in a world of confusion"? What causes this feeling for him?

_____

_____

2. Who are "my own people" for the poet?

_____

_____

3. Why does he go through this list of historical events? Which events does he include? Why these? What point is he making?

_____

_____

4. What didn't the Anglos/Europeans take from him? Why is this important to the poet?

_____

_____

5. What is his message by the end of the poem?

_____

_____

Part II

Directions: Go to http://www.chicanoparksandiego.com/murals/index.html or http://depts.washington.edu/civilr/mecha_photos.htm and pick two murals to study.

Mural 1:_____

Analyzing the Image

What objects, shapes or people do you see?

Name:_____ Date: _____

What colors does the artist use?
Are the images realistic or abstract?
What materials does the artist use? (paint, metal, wood, etc)
How does the art make you feel? Why?

Mural 2: _____

Analyzing the Image

What objects, shapes or people do you see?
What colors does the artist use?

Name:_____ Date: _____

Are the images realistic or abstract?
What materials does the artist use? (paint, metal, wood, etc)
How does the art make you feel? Why?

1. What are the major themes and topics of the murals (you can briefly look at some of the other murals on the site)?

    _____

    _____

2. What is the purpose of these murals? Why put them in such public locations outside, where they can be worn away by sun and weather?

    _____

    _____

3. How do the topics and messages of the murals fit with the ideas in the songs we listened to?

    _____

    _____

4. Based on the poem, songs, and murals, how would you summarize the goal and message of the Chicano Movement in the United States in the 1970s?

    _____

    _____

Name: _____ Date: _____

HANDOUT 3.2
Analyzing Music of the Chicano Movement

Directions: Listen to and analyze each song and answer the questions.

"Yo soy Chicano" by Los Alvarados

Lyrics	Music/Accompaniment
What is the song about? Summarize the song.	Describe the music or melody of this song. Is it fast-paced or slow? Does it have low notes or high notes? Is it melodic or does it have lots of percussion?
What are the main points of the song? What is the song saying about the subject?	
	What feelings do you get from the music? Why?
What mood/values/feelings does the singer have about the topic?	What instruments do you hear?

"El quinto sol" by Los Peludos

Lyrics	Music/Accompaniment
What is the song about? Summarize the song.	Describe the music or melody of this song. Is it fast-paced or slow? Does it have low notes or high notes? Is it melodic or does it have lots of percussion?
What are the main points of the song? What is the song saying about the subject?	
	What feelings do you get from the music? Why?
What mood/values/feelings does the singer have about the topic?	What instruments do you hear?

Handout 3.2: Analyzing Music of the Chicano Movement, continued

"Yo soy tu hermano, yo soy Chicano" by Conjunto Aztlan

Lyrics	Music/Accompaniment
What is the song about? Summarize the song.	Describe the music or melody of this song. Is it fast-paced or slow? Does it have low notes or high notes? Is it melodic or does it have lots of percussion?
What are the main points of the song? What is the song saying about the subject?	What feelings do you get from the music? Why?
What mood/values/feelings does the singer have about the topic?	What instruments do you hear?

"América de los indios" by Daniel Valdez

Lyrics	Music/Accompaniment
What is the song about? Summarize the song.	Describe the music or melody of this song. Is it fast-paced or slow? Does it have low notes or high notes? Is it melodic or does it have lots of percussion?
What are the main points of the song? What is the song saying about the subject?	What feelings do you get from the music? Why?
What mood/values/feelings does the singer have about the topic?	What instruments do you hear?

Name:_____ Date: _____

"Chicano Park Samba" by Los Alacranes Mojados

Lyrics	Music/Accompaniment
What is the song about? Summarize the song.	Describe the music or melody of this song. Is it fast-paced or slow? Does it have low notes or high notes? Is it melodic or does it have lots of percussion?
What are the main points of the song? What is the song saying about the subject?	What feelings do you get from the music? Why?
What mood/values/feelings does the singer have about the topic?	What instruments do you hear?

1. What do you notice about the music/sound of these songs? How does the sound of these songs compare to other music we have listened to from the 1970s?

   _____

   _____

2. How does the mood and message of these songs compare to the mood and message of the poem *I Am Joaquin*?

   _____

   _____

3. What elements of identity are these songs stressing and finding important? What culture and traditions are they promoting?

   _____

   _____

4. How do these songs view ethnicity and ethnic relations in the United States? What do they want to see happen?

   _____

   _____

AIM: The American Indian Movement

Alignment of Unit Goals

» Goal 1: To understand the concept of identity in 1970s America.
» Goal 2: To develop skills in historical analysis and song and artwork interpretation.
» Goal 4: To develop an understanding of historical events occurring in the United States during the 1970s.

Unit Objectives

» To describe how the American identity changed during the 1970s.
» To describe how changes in American identity in the 1970s were revealed in the music, art, and literature of the decade.
» To define the context in which a song or piece of art was produced and the implications of context for understanding the artifact.

» To describe a writer's or artist's intent in producing a given song or piece of art based on understanding of text and context.

» To describe major historical events during the 1970s that affected the American identity.

» To describe music, art, and literature of the 1970s that reflected the American identity.

Resources for Unit Implementation

» **Handout 4.1:** Native American Songs

» **Handout 4.2:** XIT Music Analysis

» **Handout 4.3:** AIM

» **Handout 2.5:** Groups Fighting for Civil Rights in the 1970s

» **Listen:** "Custer Died for Your Sins" by Floyd Red Crow Westerman (1969); and "My Country 'tis of Thy People You're Dying" by Buffy Sainte-Marie (1966). Both songs are available on YouTube.

» **Listen:** "Reservation of Education" (Bee, 1973a), "Beginnings" (Bee, 1972), and "We Live" (1973b) by XIT. All songs are available on YouTube.

» **Read and View:** Alcatraz Proclamation, available at http://www.yvwiiusdinvnohii.net/history/AlcatrazProclamation1969.htm; and picture of Alcatraz Proclamation, available at http://foundsf.org/index.php?title=ALCATRAZ_Proclamation

» **View:** AIM timeline at http://www.historyrocket.com/American-History/timeline/before-1600/american-indian/American-Indian-Movement-Timeline.html

Key Terms

» *Proclamation*: an official statement made by a person or people in power

Learning Experiences

1. **Ask:** What do you know about the Native Americans? What events can you name or remember from American history involving the Native Americans? By the 1970s, where were most Native American tribes? Why there? Do you know when Native Americans received the right to vote?

2. Tell students that today they will look at the status of Native Americans in the 1970s. Give students Handout 4.1 (Native American Songs) and listen to "Custer Died for Your Sins" by Floyd Red Crow Westerman (1969) and "My Country 'tis of Thy People You're Dying" by Buffy Sainte-Marie (1966). Discuss student responses.

3. Play the XIT song "Reservation of Education" (Bee, 1973a) and discuss student responses to the questions. Then play "Beginnings" (Bee, 1972), also by XIT. Distribute Handout 4.2 (XIT Music Analysis). **Ask:** How does "Beginnings" sound compared to other music of the 1970s? What do you notice about the sounds? Based on how they sound, does it surprise you that the same group recorded both "Beginnings" and "Reservation of Education"? Play XIT's "We Live" (Bee, 1973b). What do you notice about the music in this song? What instruments are dominant? From what culture are those instruments? What is the message of the song? Why did this group record these types of songs? What was their goal?

How are the XIT songs similar to the first two songs you listened to by Floyd Red Crow Westerman and Buffy Sainte-Marie? How are the XIT songs different? What cultural traits and traditions were all the songs promoting? What do the songs tell us about the views of Native Americans in the 1970s?

4. Explain to students that in 1968, the Native Americans formed the organization AIM, the American Indian Movement, to end the discrimination, brutality, and lack of rights faced by Native Americans. (A timeline can be found at http://www.historyrocket.com/American-History/timeline/before-1600/american-indian/American-Indian-Movement-Timeline.html.) In 1969, a group of Native Americans took over Alcatraz Island in San Francisco Bay. Give students a copy of the Alcatraz Proclamation and have students read and analyze the document using Handout 4.3 (AIM).

5. After students have read the handout, show them an image of the Alcatraz Proclamation. **Ask:** What is the proclamation about? Why did AIM use this format for their proclamation? What point were they making through the appearance of their proclamation? How did Native Americans view ethnic relationships in the United States? What did the Native Americans want to see happen for ethnic minorities?

6. Have students read the other events on the AIM timeline and complete Handout 4.3. Discuss student responses. **Ask:** What was the goal or agenda of AIM? How were the actions and goals of AIM similar to the actions and goals of the Chicano Movement? How were they different? What elements of identity were becoming more important to people? Why at that moment? How would you summarize the goals and message of Native Americans in the 1970s?

7. Have students take out their copies of Handout 2.5 (Groups Fighting for Civil Rights in the 1970s). Together, discuss responses to put in the column for the American Indian Movement. Have students save this chart; they will add to it as they go through the next several lessons.

Assessing Student Learning

- » Handout 4.1 (Native American Songs)
- » Handout 4.2 (XIT Music Analysis)
- » Handout 4.3 (AIM)
- » Handout 2.5 (Groups Fighting for Civil Rights in the 1970s)
- » Discussions

Extending Student Learning

The following are optional activities for extending student learning in this lesson:

- » Have students consider how Native Americans symbols are used as mascots in modern professional sports. Have them discuss whether they agree or disagree with using the Native Americans (as a race) for mascots (e.g., Cleveland Indians, Washington Redskins, etc.)?
- » The AIM improved public awareness of Native American issues at that time. Have students investigate the issues that are problematic for today's Native Americans.
- » Have students explore any aspect of Native American culture that interests them and then share their findings with their peers.

Name: _____ Date: _____

Directions: After listening to each song, respond to the related questions. Be prepared to share your responses with the whole group.

"Custer Died for Your Sins" by Floyd Red Crow Westerman

1. Who is Custer? Why is this song titled this way? What message is Westerman sending?

    _____

    _____

2. What treaties have been broken in the song?

    _____

    _____

3. What does Westerman mean when he says "a new day must begin"?

    _____

    _____

"My Country 'tis of Thy People You're Dying" by Buffy Sainte-Marie

1. What issues does Sainte Marie have with the traditional teaching of American history? How does she view history?

    _____

    _____

2. How does she depict Native American-White relations? Who benefits?

    _____

    _____

Summary

1. What is the message of these two songs?

    _____

    _____

Name: _____ Date: _____

HANDOUT 4.2
XIT Music Analysis

Directions: After listening to each song, respond to the related questions. Be prepared to share your responses with the whole group.

"Reservation of Education" by XIT

1. How does the sound of this song compare to other music we have listened to from the 1970s? Similarities? Differences?

    _____

    _____

2. What is the message of this song? What criticisms are the songwriters making? They compare "cowboys versus Indians" to "Washington and Indians." What does that suggest about how they see the status of Indians today?

    _____

    _____

3. What is the mood of the song?

    _____

    _____

"Beginnings" by XIT

1. What do you notice about the music and sound of this song?

    _____

    _____

"We Live" by XIT

1. What is the message of this song?

    _____

    _____

2. What instruments do you notice in this song? What cultures are those instruments from?

    _____

    _____

3. Why do you think XIT recorded songs that sound like this and used these instruments? What was their purpose?

    _____

Name: _____ Date: _____

HANDOUT 4.3
AIM

Part I

Directions: Read the Alcatraz Proclamation, and then analyze it using these questions.

1. What purpose do the writers give for being on Alcatraz? What is their offer?

_____

_____

_____

2. What is their argument about reservation lands?

_____

_____

_____

3. Why do they feel Alcatraz is a fitting location? What statement are they making to the world by taking Alcatraz?

_____

_____

_____

4. What will they do with the island? What kinds of things will they build? Why?

_____

_____

_____

5. How do the ideas in this document and their goals for Alcatraz fit with the message of the songs we just listened to?

_____

_____

_____

6. Look at a picture of the actual proclamation: Why this format? What message are they sending by presenting the proclamation this way?

_____

_____

_____

Handout 4.3: AIM, continued

Part II

Directions: Read the timeline on the AIM website at http://www.historyrocket.com/American-History/timeline/before-1600/american-indian/American-Indian-Movement-Timeline.html.

1.   What types of events are on the timeline? Why? What is AIM trying to achieve?

_____

_____

_____

2.   What is the goal or agenda of AIM?

_____

_____

_____

3.   How are these goals similar to the goals of the Chicano Movement? How are they different?

_____

_____

_____

4.   What elements of identity are becoming more important to people? Why now?

_____

_____

_____

Beyond Civil Rights: African Americans in the 1970s

Alignment of Unit Goals

> » Goal 1: To understand the concept of identity in 1970s America.
> » Goal 2: To develop skills in historical analysis and song and artwork interpretation.
> » Goal 3: To develop analytical and interpretive skills in literature.
> » Goal 4: To develop an understanding of historical events occurring in the United States during the 1970s.

Unit Objectives

> » To describe how the American identity changed during the 1970s.

» To describe how changes in American identity in the 1970s were revealed in the music, art, and literature of the decade.

» To define the context in which a song or piece of art was produced and the implications of context for understanding the artifact.

» To describe a writer's or artist's intent in producing a given song or piece of art based on understanding of text and context.

» To describe what a selected literary passage means.

» To make inferences based on information in given passages.

» To describe major historical events during the 1970s that affected the American identity.

Resources for Unit Implementation

» **Handout 5.1:** African American Identity in the 1970s

» **Handout 5.2:** African American Music in the 1970s Q & A

» **Handout 5.3:** African American Identity Chart

» **Handout 2.5:** Groups Fighting for Civil Rights in the 1970s

» **Watch:** "Soul Train: The Best of the 70s" at http://www.youtube.com/watch?v=FkleiqrWji0 (until the 2:00 mark).

» **Read:** "Everyday Use" by Alice Walker (1973/2011), available at http://xroads.virginia.edu/~ug97/quilt/walker.html

» **Read:** Excerpt from Maya Angelou's *I Know Why the Caged Bird Sings* (1969/2009), available at http://usatoday30.usatoday.com/life/books/excerpts/2004-09-22-i-know-why_x.htm?csp=34.

» **Listen:** "Black Man" (Wonder & Byrd, 1976) by Stevie Wonder; "Everyday People" (Stone, 1968) by Sly and the Family Stone; "Black Is" (Hassen, 1971) by The Last Poets. All songs available on YouTube.

Learning Experiences

1. Show students the video clip "Soul Train: The Best of the 70s" at http://www.youtube.com/watch?v=FkleiqrWji0. Watch up to the 2-minute mark, when the focus shifts to 1980s artists. Explain that *Soul Train* was a weekly show that ran from 1971–2006. The weekly broadcast featured a puzzle where an audience member had to unscramble letters to reveal the night's performer or an important person in African American history, the *Soul Train* dance line (as shown in the video), and a guest musical performer with an interview. The musical guests were predominantly R&B, soul, or hip-hop artists. **Ask:** What do you notice about the clips from *Soul Train*?

2. **Ask:** What was the state of the Civil Rights Movement by the start of the 1970s? How did *Soul Train* fit with the ideas of Black Power? What progress does this show suggest African Americans made since the early 1960s? Would a show like this have been possible 10 years earlier? Why or why not? What limitations in racial equality does the show reveal still existed in the 1970s?

3. Explain that by the 1970s, despite continuing racial inequalities, many African American musicians such as The Jackson 5, Diana Ross, Marvin Gaye, and others were part of

mainstream American music, and there were new African American writers becoming popular in American literature. Toni Morrison, Maya Angelou, and Alice Walker all wrote novels, short stories, and poems. Alex Haley published *Roots: The Saga of an American Family*, a novel that traced the history of his family from being kidnapped into slavery in Africa to the present. Tell students that they will read a story by Alice Walker (1973/2011), "Everyday Use," and an excerpt from Maya Angelou's (1969/2009) *I Know Why the Caged Bird Sings*. URLs to the story and excerpt are listed under the "Resources for Unit Implementation" section. Give students a copy of Handout 5.1 (African American Identity in the 1970s) to complete. Discuss student answers as a class. **Ask:** What do these stories reveal about African American experiences in the 1970s? What challenges do these stories reveal? What values and traits do these stories emphasize?

4. Have students listen to and analyze "Black Man" (Wonder & Byrd, 1976) by Stevie Wonder; "Everyday People" (Stone, 1968) by Sly and the Family Stone; and "Black Is" (Hassen, 1971) by The Last Poets. Have students complete Handout 5.2 (African American Music in the 1970s Q & A). Discuss student responses as a class. **Ask:** What were the overall messages and purposes of these songs? What did they seek or desire? What divisions still existed in the U.S.? Both Stevie Wonder and Sly and the Family Stone referenced other ethnic groups, why? What was their point? How do the ideas in the songs match with the stories you read?

5. Have students complete Handout 5.3 (African American Identity Chart). Discuss student responses. **Ask:** What traditions and values do you see in the stories and songs? What were they promoting and celebrating? What new views on race do you get from the stories and songs? What do the songs and stories reveal about what the economic status of some African Americans was? What racial issues still exist in the present day?

6. Have students take out their copies of Handout 2.5 (Groups Fighting for Civil Rights in the 1970s). Together, discuss responses to put in the column for the African American row. Now that the chart has been completed, hold a discussion regarding the similarities and differences among the four groups.

Assessing Student Learning

» Handout 5.1 (African American Identity in the 1970s)
» Handout 5.2 (African American Music in the 1970s Q & A)
» Handout 5.3 (African American Identity Chart)
» Handout 2.5 (Groups Fighting for Civil Rights in the 1970s)
» Discussions

Extending Student Learning

The following are optional activities for extending student learning in this lesson:

» Have students research biographical information about Maya Angelou. Then have students read aloud her poem "On the Pulse of the Morning," which she read at President Bill Clinton's inauguration in 1993 (the poem is available at http://poetry.eserver.org/angelou.html). Have students respond to these questions:

- ○ What information about Angelou's life surprises you? Why?
- ○ Which aspects of her life are reflected in the poem?
- ○ What can you infer about Angelou's feelings about America?

» Have students gather additional information about *Soul Train*, its history, and its performers. Have them present their findings in an interactive format to their classmates.

» Have students use the Rock and Roll Hall of Fame website (http://www.rockhall.com) to find the names of African American inductees. Each student may research an inductee of his or her choice and present biographical information and details about the person's contributions to the world of music.

HANDOUT 5.1

African American Identity in the 1970s

Directions: Read the stories, then respond to these questions.

"Everyday Use" by Alice Walker

1. How does Dee feel about her family, her home, and their things when she lives at home?

   _____

   _____

2. Where does Dee go? How does she achieve this?

   _____

   _____

3. When Dee/Wangero returns home, what has changed? Why has she changed her name?

   _____

   _____

4. Why does she take the pictures of her mama in the front yard? What kinds of things does she try to get in the picture? What was she trying to show? To whom?

   _____

   _____

5. Why does Wangero want the items from the house? What will she do with them? What do they mean to her? What is the significance of the fact that Maggie knows the history of the objects and who made them, and Wangero—who wants the objects—does not? What does this tell us about Wangero's feelings about the objects?

   _____

   _____

6. What will Maggie and Mama do with these same things? What do the things mean to Maggie and Mama?

   _____

   _____

7. Why does Mama take the quilts and give them to Maggie and not Wangero in the end?

   _____

   _____

Handout 5.1: African American Identity in the 1970s, continued

8. What point is the story making about African American culture in the 1970s?

_____

_____

"I Know Why the Caged Bird Sings"

1. How does the narrator envision her "real" self? What does that tell us?

_____

_____

2. How does she describe life for African Americans in the South?

_____

_____

3. Why does she tell the story about her and Bailey on the train and about the store in the mornings? What point is she making about the African American community?

_____

_____

Name: _____   Date: _____

HANDOUT 5.2

African American Music in the 1970s Q & A

Directions: Respond to these questions after listening to the songs. Be prepared to share your answers with the whole group.

"Black Man" by Stevie Wonder

1. What is going on in this song? Why are the songwriters listing all of these historical events and their creators?

    _____

    _____

2. What is the songwriters' message in this song? What are they asking for?

    _____

    _____

"Everyday People" by Sly and the Family Stone

1. What are "everyday people"?

    _____

    _____

2. What is the songwriters' message in this song?

    _____

    _____

"Black Is" by The Last Poets

1. How does this describe what "Black" is? Why are there both positive and negative images? What is the significance of these different examples?

    _____

    _____

2. What traits, values, and aspirations does the songwriter associate with "Black"?

    _____

    _____

Name:_____ Date: _____

HANDOUT 5.3

African American Identity Chart

Directions: Please complete this chart relative to the identity of African Americans in the 1970s.

<table>
<tr>
<td rowspan="4" style="writing-mode: vertical">**African American Identity in the 1970s**</td>
<td>**Race/Ethnicity:** How do the literature and songs say American notions of ethnicity affected African Americans? What views of race and ethnicity do they express?</td>
</tr>
<tr>
<td>**Culture and Traditions:** What traditions and values do the stories and songs describe? What were they trying to promote, preserve, or celebrate?</td>
</tr>
<tr>
<td>**History and Myths:** What historical events and trends are dominant in the stories and songs? What do they add to the traditional historical narrative?</td>
</tr>
<tr>
<td>**Economy:** What do the songs and stories reveal about the economic status of many African Americans in the 1970s? What divisions does this show still existed in the U.S.?</td>
</tr>
</table>

LESSON 6

The Me Decade

Alignment of Unit Goals

» Goal 1: To understand the concept of identity in 1970s America.
» Goal 2: To develop skills in historical analysis and song and artwork interpretation.
» Goal 3: To develop analytical and interpretive skills in literature.
» Goal 4: To develop an understanding of historical events occurring in the United States during the 1970s.

Unit Objectives

» To describe how the American identity changed during the 1970s.
» To describe how changes in American identity in the 1970s were revealed in the music, art, and literature of the decade.
» To define the context in which a song or piece of art was produced and the implications of context for understanding the artifact.
» To describe a writer's or artist's intent in producing a given song or piece of art based on understanding of text and context.

» To describe what a selected literary passage means.
» To make inferences based on information in given passages.
» To describe major historical events during the 1970s that affected the American identity.
» To describe music, art, and literature of the 1970s that reflected the American identity.

Resources for Unit Implementation

» **Handout 6.1:** Comparing Groups of the 1970s Venn Diagram
» **Handout 6.2:** Me Decade
» **Handout 6.3:** The Melting Pot Q & A
» **Handout 6.4:** Art Analysis Model: Postmodern Architecture
» **Handout 6.5:** Primary Source Document Analysis Model
» **Read:** Excerpts from *Jonathan Livingston Seagull* (Bach, 1970/2006), available at http://www.conures.net/stories/seagull.shtml
» **Listen:** "We Are the Champions" (Mercury, 1977) by Queen; "Lookin' Out for #1" (Bachman, 1975) by Bachman-Turner Overdrive. Both songs are available on YouTube.
» **Listen:** "You're So Vain" by Carly Simon (1972); "Life's Been Good" by Joe Walsh (1978). Both songs are available on YouTube.
» **Watch:** *Schoolhouse Rock!* "The Great American Melting Pot" segment at http://www.youtube.com/watch?v=-__GGvzmfXQ.
» **View:** Picture of Charles Moore's (1974–1978) Piazza d'Italia: http://www.neworleansonline.com/images/slideshows/listings/1344/05.jpg
» **View:** Picture of Carlo Scarpa's (1968–1978) Brion Cemetery: http://www.greatbuildings.com/buildings/Brion-Vega_Cemetery.html
» **View:** Picture of Hans Hollein's (1972–1982) Abteiberg Museum: http://www.hollein.com/eng/Architecture/Nations/Germany/Staedtisches-Museum-Abteiberg
» **View:** Summary of *U.S. v. Nixon*: http://newshour-tc.pbs.org/newshour/extra/wp-content/uploads/sites/2/2013/11/U-S-v-Nixon.pdf
» **View:** Transcript excerpt from June 23, 1972, Nixon White House tapes: http://newshour-tc.pbs.org/newshour/extra/wp-content/uploads/sites/2/2013/11/Smoking-Gun-Transcript-v-2.pdf

Key Terms

» *Self-help:* the process of doing things to improve one's self or to solve one's problems without getting help from others
» *Postmodern architecture:* a term that is used to describe the architecture of buildings that integrate modernism with some classical or neoclassical elements; the postmodern movement in architecture began in the 1970s

Learning Experiences

1. **Ask:** What groups have you been discussing during this unit? Have students get out their chart from Lesson 2 and use what they have learned to complete the Venn diagram of

the four groups in Handout 6.1. Have students consider the cultural traits, values, experiences, history, views, methods, goals, and expressions. **Ask:** What did these groups all have in common in the 1970s?

2. Explain to students that in the 1970s, not only were ethnic groups expressing their individuality, but there was an increase in the number of "self-help" books that focused on individual needs. **Ask:** Do you know what a self-help book is? A book called *I'm OK— You're OK* (Harris, 1967/2004) topped the best-seller lists in the early 1970s. What does the title alone suggest about the message of the book? How does the title *I'm OK—You're OK* fit with the ideas in the songs and literature you have been studying of the four groups in our Venn diagram?

3. Tell students another popular title was *Jonathan Livingston Seagull* (Bach, 1970/2006), which was about a seagull learning about life and flying. Give students the excerpts and Handout 6.2 (Me Decade) to complete individually or in small groups. Discuss student responses. **Ask:** According to *Jonathan Livingston Seagull*, where is knowledge? What keeps you from being happy? What is the book encouraging you to do?

4. Have students listen to "We Are the Champions" (Mercury, 1977) by Queen and "Lookin' Out for #1" (Bachman, 1975) by Bachman-Turner Overdrive and answer the second set of questions in Handout 6.2. **Ask:** What is good about following the advice/messages of these songs and books? What might be the negative consequences?

5. Explain that two popular songs of the early 1970s might help us think about the negative side of the dominant focus on the self. Have students listen to "You're So Vain" by Carly Simon (1972), which was a top 10 hit in 1974, and "Life's Been Good" by Joe Walsh (1978). Have students answer the third set of questions in Handout 6.2. Discuss student responses as a whole class. **Ask:** Which elements of identity were becoming more important to people in the 1970s? Why? How did political, economic, and social events explain this? Do you think the "Me Decade" was an appropriate name for this decade given what you have learned so far? Why or why not?

6. **Ask:** What experiences and conditions were changing how Americans expressed themselves? Why was there such a focus on expressing one's individuality and looking out for one's self? What values and beliefs did each individual still hold in common in America? What common values were revealed in the fact that everyone wanted to celebrate his or her culture and individuality? Can people look out for themselves without trampling others?

7. Tell students that during the 1970s on Saturday mornings, *Schoolhouse Rock!* segments would appear to teach kids about grammar, science, math, and social issues. Show students the *Schoolhouse Rock!* "Melting Pot" segment at http://www.youtube.com/ watch?v=-__GGvzmfXQ and answer the questions in Handout 6.3 (The Melting Pot Q & A). **Ask:** How is the "melting pot" an accurate and good metaphor for the United States? Why is it an attractive way to think about our country? How is the idea of a melting pot a negative or problematic depiction of our culture? How do the groups you have been studying currently feel like the melting pot has affected their culture? What were ethnic groups in the 1970s asking for?

8. **Discuss the following:** What are contributions or cultural traits of different ethnic groups you can see in your own community? How and where do you see different ethnic groups

expressing their culture, and what makes them unique? What traits do people still share that unify them as Americans?

9. Introduce the idea of postmodern architecture to students. Show them examples of works by the architects listed under "Resources for Unit Implementation" and have them analyze one work of architecture using Handout 6.3 (Art Analysis Model: Postmodern Architecture).

10. Finally, explain that Watergate was an important event in the 1970s that shaped American politics, the Office of the President, and how the media worked with the White House. Tell students that the Watergate scandal exemplified politicians' own self-interest and started to breed public distrust in the government and in federal affairs. Introduce Watergate by having students read the summary of *U.S. v. Nixon* and the excerpt from the June 23, 1972, Nixon White House tapes. Have them complete Handout 6.5 (Primary Source Document Analysis Model) after reading the transcript excerpts. Hold a whole-class discussion about the limits of presidential power in the United States.

Assessing Student Learning

» Handout 6.1 (Comparing Groups of the 1970s Venn Diagram)
» Handout 6.2 (Me Decade)
» Handout 6.3: (The Melting Pot Q & A)
» Handout 6.4 (Art Analysis Model: Postmodern Architecture)
» Handout 6.5 (Primary Source Document Analysis Model)
» Discussions

Extending Student Learning

The following are optional activities for extending student learning in this lesson:

» Have students conduct additional research about the postmodern movement in architecture that began in the 1970s. They should collect pictures of buildings designed during the period and provide information about the architects.

» Have interested students read all of *Jonathan Livingston Seagull* (Bach, 1970/2006). Each student should develop a music playlist representing the four key parts of the book, then share it with his or her classmates and provide commentary about the music chosen.

» Have students write "self-help" books (or booklets) to address common problems of middle school students. Students should conduct research to substantiate the recommendations they make in the books.

» Have students research another presidential scandal, such as Iran-Contra, Whitewater, or the Lewinsky-Clinton scandal. Have students explore the influence of Watergate on the media's investigation of these scandals and their willingness to investigate the president of the United States.

» Have students investigate Ford's pardon of Nixon, including the reasons behind it and its consequences.

Name: _____ Date: _____

Comparing Groups of the 1970s Venn Diagram

Directions: Compare the four groups you have studied so far in this unit. Use the Venn diagram to compare the cultural traits, values, experiences, history, views, methods, goals, and expressions of each group.

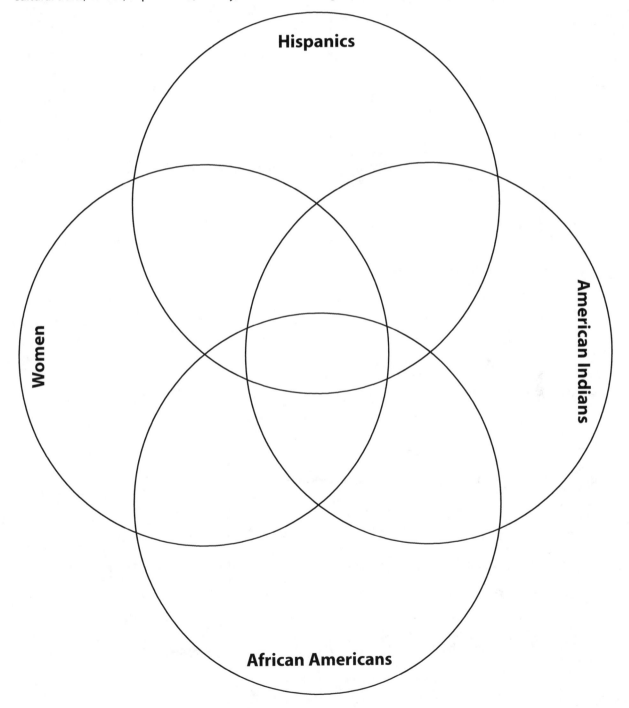

Name: _____ Date: _____

HANDOUT 6.2
Me Decade

Directions: Respond to these questions after reading the excerpts and listening to various songs from the 1970s.

Jonathan Livingston Seagull

1. What is your reaction to these excerpts? Why?

   _____

   _____

2. Where is knowledge according to these readings? What do we need to move forward?

   _____

   _____

3. According to the book, why do most people not achieve happiness? Why are most people held back? Who is responsible for your success and future?

   _____

   _____

4. What are these passages encouraging you to do?

   _____

   _____

"We Are the Champions" and "Lookin' Out for #1"

1. What is the topic of these songs? Was their path easy? How did they achieve success?

   _____

   _____

2. How are these songs similar to the ideas in *Jonathan Livingston Seagull*? Different?

   _____

   _____

3. Which seems to be more important in these songs and books: individual needs or national identity? Why?

   _____

   _____

4. Given what we know about life in 1970s U.S., why might these ideas have been attractive to people?

   _____

   _____

Handout 6.2: Me Decade, continued

"You're So Vain" and "Life's Been Good"

1. What are the negative consequences of the focus on self and your own success as seen in these songs? What might be some other negative consequences?

_____

_____

Summary

1. What elements of identity were more important to people in the 1970s? Why? How might political, economic, and social events explain this?

_____

_____

2. Do you think the "Me Decade" is an appropriate name for this decade given what we have learned so far? Why or why not?

_____

_____

HANDOUT 6.3
Melting Pot Q & A

Directions: Respond to the following questions.

1. What historical events and values does the *Schoolhouse Rock!* song stress as common identity traits of Americans? Why did the song mention these particular events and values?

   _____

   _____

2. The song says, "no matter your skin, doesn't matter where you're from." Do you think the groups we have studied so far agreed with this statement? Why or why not?

   _____

   _____

3. Later the song says, "How great to be an American and something else as well." How does this fit with the ideas we have been hearing from the Chicano movement, African American literature, AIM, and even self-help books?

   _____

   _____

4. How is a "melting pot" an accurate metaphor for the United States? Why is it an attractive way to think about our country?

   _____

   _____

5. How is the idea of a melting pot a negative or problematic depiction of our culture? How do the groups we have been studying currently feel the "melting pot" has affected their culture? What were ethnic groups in the 1970s asking for?

   _____

   _____

6. Can you think of a better metaphor for America and American identity than a melting pot? What would it be and why?

   _____

   _____

Name: _____ Date: _____

HANDOUT 6.4

Art Analysis Model:
Postmodern Architecture

Directions: Analyze one of the images of postmodern architecture provided. Be prepared to share your responses with your classmates.

Architect: _____
Work/Building: _____

What is the title of the artwork? Why was it given this title?

Title:
Why do you think it was given this title?
Which words in the title are especially important? Why?
What does the title reveal about the artwork?

What do you see in the artwork?

What objects, shapes, or people do you see?
What colors does the artist use? Why?
Are the images in the work realistic or abstract?
What materials does the artist use? Why?

What is your reaction to the image?

What is the first thing about this image that draws your attention?
What is in the image that surprises you, or that you didn't expect?

Name: _____ Date: _____

| What are some of the powerful ideas expressed in the image? |
| What feelings does the image cause in you? |
| What questions does it raise for you? |

When was the image produced? Why was it produced?

| Who is the artist? |
| When was the artwork produced? |
| What were the important events occurring at the time the artwork was produced? |
| What was the author's purpose in producing this artwork? |
| Who is the intended audience? |

What are the important ideas in this artwork?

| What assumptions/values/feelings are reflected in the artwork? |
| What are the artist's views about the issue(s)? |

What is your evaluation of this artwork?

| What new or different interpretation of this historical period does this artwork provide? |
| What does this artwork portray about American identity or how Americans felt at the time? |

Name: _____ Date: _____

HANDOUT 6.5

Primary Source Document Analysis Model

Directions: Use the transcript excerpt from the June 23, 1972, White House tapes to complete the following chart.

Document: _____

What is the title of the document? Why was it given this title?

Title:
Why do you think it was given this title?
Which words in the title are especially important? Why?

What is your reaction to the document?

What is the first thing about this document that draws your attention?

Name:_____ Date: _____

What is in the document that surprises you, or that you didn't expect?
What are some of the powerful ideas expressed in the document?
What feelings does the primary source cause in you?
What questions does it raise for you?

When was the document written? Why was it written?

Who is the author(s)?
When was the document written?

Name:_____ Date:_____

What do you know about the culture of the time period in which the document was written?
What were the important events occurring at the time the document was written?
What was the author's purpose in writing this document?
Who is the intended audience?
What biases do you see in the author's text?

What are the important ideas in this document?

What problems or events does the document address?

Name: _____ Date: _____

What is the author's main point or argument?

What actions or outcomes does the author expect? From whom?

How do you think this author would define *American identity*? What elements of the American identity does the author see as being threatened or cultivated? Why?

What is your evaluation of this document?

Is this document authentic? How do you know?

Is this author a reliable source for addressing this issue/problem?

How representative is this document of the views of the people at this time in history?

Name:_____ Date:_____

How does this document compare with others of the same time period?
What could have been the possible consequences of this document?
What actually happened as a result of this document? Discuss the long-term, short-term, and unintended consequences.
What interpretation of this historical period does this document provide?
How does this document contribute to your understanding of the American identity during this time period?

LESSON 7

Lines at the Gas Station: The Oil Crisis

Alignment of Unit Goals

» Goal 1: To understand the concept of identity in 1970s America.
» Goal 2: To develop skills in historical analysis and song and artwork interpretation.
» Goal 4: To develop an understanding of historical events occurring in the United States during the 1970s.

Unit Objectives

» To describe how the American identity changed during the 1970s.
» To describe how changes in American identity in the 1970s were revealed in the music, art, and literature of the decade.
» To define the context in which a song or piece of art was produced and the implications of context for understanding the artifact.

» To describe a writer's or artist's intent in producing a given song or piece of art based on understanding of text and context.

» To describe major historical events during the 1970s that affected the American identity.

» To describe music, art, and literature of the 1970s that reflected the American identity.

Resources for Unit Implementation

» **Handout 7.1:** Gas Lines

» **Handout 7.2:** Identity Chart

» **Handout 7.3:** Role of American Citizens in Crisis

» **Handout 7.4:** Identity During the Energy Crisis

» **Listen:** "President Nixon, Don't Ration My Gas" by Diana Gardiner (1973); "The Crude Oil Blues" by Jerry Reed (1974). Gardiner's song is available at http://blog.wfmu.org/freeform/2006/05/songs_of_bygone.html, and Reed's song is available on YouTube.

» **Listen:** "Cheaper Crude or No More Food" (Burns, 1979) by Bobby Butler; "The Americans" (Sinclair, 1974) by Byron MacGregor. Both songs are available on YouTube.

» **Watch:** *Schoolhouse Rock!* video "The Energy Blues" at http://www.youtube.com/watch?v=8rrgpGo1Fw8

» **Listen:** "There's Only So Much Oil in the Ground" (Castillo & Kupka, 1975) By Tower of Power. Available on YouTube.

Key Terms

» *Crude oil:* a naturally occurring, unrefined petroleum product

» *Embargo:* a government order that limits trade in some manner

» *Ration:* to restrict the distribution and/or consumption of some product

Learning Experiences

1. Have students list all of the things they use on a daily basis that use energy, either electricity or gasoline. Make a list on the board. **Ask:** What would happen if the cost of energy went up by 70%? A $3.50 gallon of gasoline would cost $5.95. How might your life change if energy became that much more expensive? What if you could only get gas for your car on odd days of the month? How might that change how you live your life? What if you went to the gas station and there was no gas?

2. Explain to students that by the mid-1970s, all of these things were happening. Gasoline went from $0.36 per gallon in 1972 to $0.61 in 1976, a 70% increase. Have students use their textbooks to summarize the Yom Kippur War and the Organization of the Petroleum Exporting Countries' (OPEC) embargo of fuel to the United States. OPEC both raised the price on oil and reduced how much it would sell to the U.S., resulting in oil shortages and increased prices. Laws were passed that if a person's license plate ended in an odd number, he or she could only get gas on odd-numbered days; gas shortages made gas stations run out of gasoline, and people would wait in line for hours to get gas. Have students consider what they know about the 1970s and refer back to the mood of the songs

they examined in the first lesson. **Ask:** What problems were people already facing and how did this energy crisis affect them?

3. Explain to students that in this lesson, they will look at the reaction of Americans to the energy crisis and how it affected people. Have students listen to Diana Gardiner's (1973) "President Nixon, Don't Ration My Gas" and Jerry Reed's (1974) "The Crude Oil Blues" and answer the questions on Handout 7.1 (Gas Lines). Discuss student responses. **Ask:** How do the songs show how the energy crisis affected people's lives? How was the ordinary person feeling the effects of the energy crisis? What is the mood of these songs? Who did the songwriters blame for the problems? Why?

4. Have students listen to Bobby Butler's "Cheaper Crude or No More Food" (Burns, 1979) and Byron MacGregor's "The Americans" (Sinclair, 1974) and complete Handout 7.2 (Identity Chart) based on all the songs. Discuss student responses. **Ask:** How do the songs view the role of citizens in this crisis? What does it tell us about American values that Americans waited in lines and sacrificed, but did not revolt or rebel? What was the effect of the energy crisis on the economy? How might the feelings in the songs have affected American views of other countries?

5. Explain that the energy crisis and rising energy prices affected Americans' views of themselves, their behavior, and the world. Watch the *Schoolhouse Rock!* segment "The Energy Blues" at http://www.youtube.com/watch?v=8rrgpGo1Fw8 and listen to Tower of Power's "There's Only So Much Oil in the Ground" (Castillo & Kupka, 1975). **Ask:** What is the message of these two songs? What is the mood of each? What do these songs say the role of an American citizen in this crisis was? How are these songs similar to messages you hear in advertising and public awareness campaigns today? Different? Have students complete Handout 7.3 (Role of American Citizens in Crisis).

6. Discuss or have students complete Handout 7.4 (Identity During the Energy Crisis) and discuss student responses. **Ask:** What do you think are the long-term effects of our current energy use? Is the U.S. still as dependent on foreign oil as it was in the 1970s? How does this affect American international relations today?

Assessing Student Learning

- » Handout 7.1 (Gas Lines)
- » Handout 7.2 (Identity Chart)
- » Handout 7.3 (Role of American Citizens in Crisis)
- » Handout 7.4 (Identity During the Energy Crisis)
- » Discussions

Extending Student Learning

The following are optional activities for extending student learning in this lesson:

- » The 1979 oil crisis was related to the Iranian Revolution. Have students research this event and present their findings about its effects on the U.S.

» Have students investigate information about the U.S.'s current domestic production of oil and its reliance on other countries for it. They should present their findings in chart or graph form.

» Have students research contemporary automobile engineering in the U.S. relative to innovations designed to reduce fuel consumption. Students should present their findings in the form of recommendations for the most fuel-efficient automobiles.

» Have students research the long-term environmental impact of the Exxon Valdez disaster on the ecology of Alaska's Prince William Sound.

» Students may investigate the current technology used in combating oil spills. Have them present their findings in an interactive format.

Name: _____   Date: _____

HANDOUT 7.1

Gas Lines

Directions: Listen to Diana Gardiner's "President Nixon Don't You Ration My Gas" and Jerry Reed's "The Crude Oil Blues" and answer the following questions.

1. How is the energy crisis changing or affecting people's daily lives in these songs? How did the ordinary person feel the effects of the energy crisis?

   _____

   _____

   _____

2. What is the mood of these songs?

   _____

   _____

   _____

3. Who do the songwriters blame for the problems? Why?

   _____

   _____

   _____

Name: _____ Date: _____

HANDOUT 7.2
Identity Chart

Directions: You have listened to four songs about the energy crisis. Complete the chart based on ideas from these songs.

Energy Crisis of the 1970s	**Civic Identity:** How do the songs view the role of citizens in this situation? According to the songs, what were our duties and responsibilities? What does it tell us that Americans waited in lines and cut back but did not revolt?
	History and Myths: What events in history do the songs mention? Why these?
	Economy: What was the effect of these events on the economy? What do the songs mention about effects on wages and businesses? Think of all of the businesses that use energy or rely on people commuting to them.
	International Role: What do the songs say about the United States' role in the world? How did we view our role in the world at this point? How did the songs suggest we should change our relations with other countries? How do you think these feelings affected American's views of other countries?

HANDOUT 7.3

Role of American Citizens in Crisis

Direction: After listening to Tower of Power's "There's Only So Much Oil in the Ground" and watching the *Schoolhouse Rock!* "The Energy Blues" video, respond to the following questions.

1. What is the message of these two songs? What is the mood of each?

    _____

    _____

    _____

2. What do these songs say is the role of an American citizen in this crisis?

    _____

    _____

    _____

3. How are these two songs and their messages similar to the environmental readings and songs we looked at in the 1960s? How are they different? (Think about mood, issues, focus, tone.)

    _____

    _____

    _____

4. How are these songs similar to messages you hear in advertising and public awareness campaigns today? How are they different?

    _____

    _____

    _____

5. How did the energy crisis in the 1970s affect American identity? How did this change our view of our roles and our relationship to our resources? How do we still see these ideas and values today?

    _____

    _____

    _____

Name:_____   Date:_____

HANDOUT 7.4

Identity During the Energy Crisis

Directions: Complete the chart based on the materials discussed in this lesson.

Identity changes with new ideas, experiences, conditions, or in response to other expressions of identity.
How did the energy crisis affect the identity of Americans? What new traits have we since adopted? How did it alter our view of our country? How did it change our view of resources and our relationship with those natural resources?

Identity is created by a group, person, or outsiders, and self-created identities may be different from how others see one's self.
In the songs, America is described as a do-gooder or caretaker of the world. Why? Is this entirely accurate? Can you think of actions by the U.S. prior to the 1970s that were not helpful or supportive of other countries? What identity did we create of ourselves and why? How did other countries view us? How did these different views of America's role in the world explain the energy crisis of the 1970s?

How did the energy crisis alter America's view of itself and how we viewed other countries? What were the consequences of this change for the future? |

Name:_____ Date:_____

Although members of a group or society may have different individual identities, they still share particular elements of identity.
What traits and values did Americans still share despite the crisis and the trouble the energy crisis brought? What beliefs do we show we still share?

LESSON 8

1976:
The Bicentennial

Alignment of Unit Goals

» Goal 1: To understand the concept of identity in 1970s America.
» Goal 2: To develop skills in historical analysis and song and artwork interpretation.
» Goal 3: To develop analytical and interpretive skills in literature.
» Goal 4: To develop an understanding of historical events occurring in the United States during the 1970s.

Unit Objectives

» To describe how the American identity changed during the 1970s.
» To describe how changes in American identity in the 1970s were revealed in the music, art, and literature of the decade.
» To define the context in which a song or piece of art was produced and the implications of context for understanding the artifact.
» To describe a writer's or artist's intent in producing a given song or piece of art based on understanding of text and context.

» To describe what a selected literary passage means.
» To make inferences based on information in given passages.
» To describe major historical events during the 1970s that affected the American identity.
» To describe music, art, and literature of the 1970s that reflected the American identity.

Resources for Unit Implementation

» **Handout 8.1:** Events for the Bicentennial
» **Watch:** 1976 Super Bowl X Half-Time Show featuring the song, "200 Years and Just a Baby," available at http://www.youtube.com/watch?v=VMBFpDm1YDE (the song begins at the 3:25 mark and ends at the 10:30 mark)
» **Watch:** Roy Rogers and Dale Evans singing, "Happy Birthday, America," available at http://www.youtube.com/watch?v=GHhtgdnVG6c.
» **Read:** President Ford's July 4th Address, available at http://www.commandposts.com/2011/07/independence-day-1976-president-gerald-ford-and-the-bicentennial/.
» **Watch:** Disney's "America on Parade" video, available at http://www.youtube.com/watch?v=Hxqt1vNtxLU, and the *Schoolhouse Rock!* video, "Fireworks," available at http://www.youtube.com/watch?v=ZTY0V8GaeFI.
» **Read:** National Coalition to Save Our Mall 1976 Bicentennial Celebration by George Idelson (2010), available at http://www.savethemall.org/moments/idelson.html

Key Terms

» *Bicentennial:* a 200th anniversary and/or its celebration
» *Coalition:* a group of people who have joined together to achieve a common purpose

Learning Experiences

1. **Ask:** What are the major events we have studied from 1970 to the end of 1975? How would you summarize the mood in the United States by the end of 1975? What was the country like?

2. Tell students that 1976 was the bicentennial of the United States, the 200th anniversary of the Declaration of Independence. Give students Handout 8.1 (Events for the Bicentennial). Tell them that the year began with Super Bowl X in January. The halftime show included a song called "200 Years and Just a Baby." Show students the clip on YouTube. Have students answer the questions about the song.

3. Show students the clip of Roy Rogers and Dale Evans singing at a Fourth of July celebration in Los Angeles and have students answer the questions on Handout 8.1. Discuss student responses. **Ask:** Based on these two songs, what was the mood of Americans at the Bicentennial? What issues did they face? What united them?

4. Have students in small groups read President Ford's July 4th Address. Next, have them watch the promo video for the Disney parade, which ran from 1975–1976 in both Disney parks, and the *Schoolhouse Rock!* video, "Fireworks," which was written specifically for the Bicentennial. Tell students to complete the chart in Handout 8.1.

5. **Ask:** How did all of these events view the future of the U.S.? Why?
   - ○ How did they fit with the Super Bowl show and the Roy Rogers and Dale Evans song?
   - ○ What is similar about them all? What traits or events do they stress that are similar?
   - ○ How do these five Bicentennial events differ? In their mood or outlook? In the type of event? Why might this have been? How do the audience and purpose of each explain the differences?
   - ○ Based on what we have learned, how do you think the American people responded to or felt about these different events tied to the Bicentennial? Why?
   - ○ What do all of these things created for the Bicentennial tell us about the U.S. in 1976, how Americans viewed themselves, and the mood of the country?
   - ○ Do you think every group in the U.S. that we have studied agreed with the views of these songs and events? Which ones? Why or why not?

6. Display the column from the National Coalition to Save Our Mall website (Idelson, 2010) for students to read. **Ask:** How does the author describe the importance of the Bicentennial? Based on the songs, parades, speech, and events we looked at, do you agree with his assessment of the Bicentennial? Do you agree that this was an important event in healing our divisions and pulling the country back together? Why or why not?

7. **Ask:** What can we conclude about American identity from the Bicentennial celebrations? How was the Bicentennial important in American history? What parts of American identity did it stress and how was this important at this time in the U.S.? How does it change or affect American identity or your view of America in the 1970s?

Assessing Student Learning

- » Handout 8.1 (Events for the Bicentennial)
- » Discussions

Extending Student Learning

The following are optional activities for extending student learning in this lesson:
- » Have students conduct research about the Declaration of Independence and its authors. Have students present the information in an interactive format to their classmates.
- » Individually or in small groups, have students write newspaper articles that might have been written to announce the Declaration of Independence and explain its most significant features to the public.
- » Have students prepare a simulated TV talk show, where each person serves as an expert about some aspect of the Constitution or the political situation in which it was written. The students may record the show, or conduct it "live" and seek audience participation.
- » Have students develop an engaging way to tell the story of the Bill of Rights and how the first 10 amendments came into existence.
- » Students may "plan" for the tercentennial (300th anniversary) of the signing of the Declaration of Independence. They should develop a program, including speakers and performers.

Name: _____ Date: _____

HANDOUT 8.1
Events for the Bicentennial

Directions: Complete the questions and the chart as you view video clips, listen to songs, and read materials about the Bicentennial.

Super Bowl X: "200 Years and Just a Baby"

1. How does this song portray the U.S.? Why choose this image? Why might this be an attractive image?

   _____

   _____

   _____

2. The song says, "Growin' like a weed, kind of rough, kinda wild." What does this suggest about the state of the U.S.? Do you think most Americans would think of their country this way? Why or why not?

   _____

   _____

   _____

3. Later it says, "Nothing's lost as long as something's learned." What is the message being sent?

   _____

   _____

   _____

4. How would you summarize the mood of this song?

   _____

   _____

   _____

Roy Rogers and Dale Evans: "Happy Birthday, America"

1. How do Rogers and Evans see the U.S. in 1976? What do they feel unifies us? What historical events do they mention?

   _____

   _____

2. What is the mood of this song?

   _____

   _____

Handout 8.1: Events for the Bicentennial, continued

3. Use President Ford's July 4th Address, Disney's "America on Parade" video, and the *Schoolhouse Rock!* video, "Fireworks," to complete the chart and answer the following questions.

	President Ford's Address	**"America on Parade"**	**"Fireworks"**
What is the mood?			
What historical events or people does it mention?			
What cultural traits of the U.S. does it mention?			
What progress does this describe in the U.S.?			
What challenges or short-comings does the U.S. have?			

How do these events view the future of the U.S.? Why? How do they fit with the Super Bowl show and the Roy Rogers and Dale Evans song? How are they all similar and how are they different? Why?

_____

_____

_____

_____

_____

LESSON 9

Saturday Night Fever: The Age of Disco

Alignment of Unit Goals

» Goal 1: To understand the concept of identity in 1970s America.

» Goal 2: To develop skills in historical analysis and song and artwork interpretation.

» Goal 4: To develop an understanding of historical events occurring in the United States during the 1970s.

Unit Objectives

» To describe how the American identity changed during the 1970s.

» To describe how changes in American identity in the 1970s were revealed in the music, art, and literature of the decade.

» To define the context in which a song or piece of art was produced and the implications of context for understanding the artifact.

» To describe a writer's or artist's intent in producing a given song or piece of art based on understanding of text and context.

» To describe major historical events during the 1970s that affected the American identity.

» To describe music, art, and literature of the 1970s that reflected the American identity.

Resources for Unit Implementation

» **Handout 9.1:** Disco Music Analysis

» **Handout 9.2:** Music in the 1970s Venn Diagram

» **Watch:** Clips from the film *Saturday Night Fever*. First, the "Night Fever" line dance, available at http://www.youtube.com/watch?v=N6IgSRGIScs. Next, the "You Should Be Dancing" clip, available at http://www.youtube.com/watch?v=Yu8z1DIMe9Q.

» **Listen:** "Night Fever" (Gibb, Gibb, & Gibb, 1977) by the Bee Gees; "Boogie Wonderland" (Willis & Lind, 1979) by Earth, Wind and Fire; "I Love the Night Life" (Bridges & Hutcheson, 1978) by Alicia Bridges; "All Night Dancin'" (Jackson & Jackson, 1978) or "Blame It on the Boogie" (Jackson, Jackson, & Elmar, 1978) by The Jacksons; and "Last Dance" (Jabara, 1978) by Donna Summer. All songs available on YouTube.

» **View:** Top 10 Songs of Each Year (1970–1974), available at http://www.digitaldreamdoor.com/pages/best_songs70-79.html

Key Terms

» *Disco:* popular dance music characterized by a pulsating rhythm, electronically produced sounds, and repetitive lyrics

» *Inflation:* a rise in prices related to an increase in the volume of money, resulting in the devaluing of a country's currency

Learning Experiences

1. Start the lesson by showing students the following two clips from the movie, *Saturday Night Fever*: "Night Fever" line dance and "You Should Be Dancing." Both scenes can be found on YouTube. **Ask:** How many of you had this image of the 1970s before starting this unit? Why is that? Explain to students that disco started to increase in popularity from the mid-1970s into the late 1970s and the movie they saw clips from, *Saturday Night Fever*, was released in 1977. What do you notice about the dancing? How does the style of the dancing fit with the ideas and values you have been discussing in this unit?

2. Give students Handout 9.1 (Disco Music Analysis) and have them analyze "Night Fever" (Gibb, Gibb, & Gibb, 1977) by the Bee Gees; "Boogie Wonderland" (Willis & Lind, 1979) by Earth, Wind and Fire; "I Love the Night Life" (Bridges & Hutcheson, 1978) by Alicia Bridges; "All Night Dancin'" (Jackson & Jackson, 1978) or "Blame It on the Boogie" (Jackson, Jackson, & Elmar, 1978) by The Jacksons; and "Last Dance" (Jabara, 1978) by Donna Summer. **Ask:** What message do these songs have in common? What did disco and disco dancing provide to people in the 1970s?

3. Provide students with the lists of the Top 10 Songs of the Year from 1970–1974. **Ask:** Which of these songs have you already listened to and discussed? Have students pick three to four other top songs from the beginning of the decade to listen and find the lyrics to. Have students compare disco to early 1970s music using Handout 9.2 (Music in the 1970s Venn Diagram) and then answer the questions. **Ask:** What stylistic differences do you hear in the music? How do the differences in the music reflect changes in American culture during the 1970s?

4. Before discussing student responses to the questions, use your textbook to review the events of the second half of the 1970s and the Carter Presidency. Explain that after President Nixon resigned, Gerald Ford was president until 1976. During his presidency, unemployment and inflation both increased, and the country went into a recession that Ford was unable to change. In 1976, Jimmy Carter was elected president. The economy continued to struggle with high unemployment and inflation, American factories were becoming less globally competitive, and Chrysler faced bankruptcy. In 1977, there was a severe winter which, combined with OPEC raising oil prices, created fuel shortages for the second time in the decade. During this time, President Carter also worked out the Camp David Accords, ending a 30-year state of war between Israel and Egypt, and negotiated SALT II, an arms limitation treaty with the Soviet Union. **Ask:** How did these events affect Americans and change life in the United States? How did these events unite Americans? Divide Americans? How might Americans feel about themselves? About their government?

5. Tell students that although these events were happening, disco was gaining in popularity through 1980. **Ask:**
   ○ What seems to have been the message of many disco songs?
   ○ How did the events in the United States and around the world explain why disco music and disco dancing were so popular at this time?
   ○ How did disco and disco dancing fit with the ideas of the "Me Decade" that you have discussed earlier in the unit?
   ○ Which elements of identity were more important to young Americans by the end of the 1970s? Why?

6. **Ask:** Thinking back to all that you have discussed about the 1970s, why is disco one of the enduring images of this decade? Why do many people think of disco when they think of the 1970s? Do you think this is an accurate image of the decade? Why or why not? What can you conclude about life in the United States in the 1970s? Describe the identity of the U.S. at this time.

Assessing Student Learning

» Handout 9.1 (Disco Music Analysis)
» Handout 9.2 (Music in the 1970s Venn Diagram)
» Discussions

Extending Student Learning

The following are optional activities for extending student learning in this lesson:

» Have students research the relationship of disco to the movements/struggles for equal rights of various groups during the 1970s. Have them respond to these questions:
  ○ In what ways did disco contribute to these movements/struggles?
  ○ In what ways did it harm the movements/struggles?

» Students may research the types of music/lyrics that reflect the movements/struggles for equal rights of various groups during the 1970s. Have students present their findings through use of the musical selections that they review.

» Have students compare disco to a contemporary style of music. They should present their findings in an interactive format.

HANDOUT 9.1
Disco Music Analysis

Directions: Analyze the songs from the Disco era.

"Night Fever" by the Bee Gees

Lyrics	Music/Accompaniment
What is the song about? Summarize the song.	Describe the music or melody of this song. Is it fast-paced or slow? Does it have low notes or high notes? Is it melodic or does it have lots of percussion?
What are the main points of the song? What is the song saying about the subject?	
	What feelings do you get from the music? Why?
What mood/values/feelings does the singer have about the topic?	What instruments do you hear?

"Boogie Wonderland" by Earth, Wind and Fire

Lyrics	Music/Accompaniment
What is the song about? Summarize the song.	Describe the music or melody of this song. Is it fast-paced or slow? Does it have low notes or high notes? Is it melodic or does it have lots of percussion?
What are the main points of the song? What is the song saying about the subject?	
	What feelings do you get from the music? Why?
What mood/values/feelings does the singer have about the topic?	What instruments do you hear?

Name:_____ Date:_____

"I Love the Nightlife" by Alicia Bridges

Lyrics	Music/Accompaniment
What is the song about? Summarize the song.	Describe the music or melody of this song. Is it fast-paced or slow? Does it have low notes or high notes? Is it melodic or does it have lots of percussion?
What are the main points of the song? What is the song saying about the subject?	What feelings do you get from the music? Why?
What mood/values/feelings does the singer have about the topic?	What instruments do you hear?

"Blame It on the Boogie" by The Jacksons

Lyrics	Music/Accompaniment
What is the song about? Summarize the song.	Describe the music or melody of this song. Is it fast-paced or slow? Does it have low notes or high notes? Is it melodic or does it have lots of percussion?
What are the main points of the song? What is the song saying about the subject?	What feelings do you get from the music? Why?
What mood/values/feelings does the singer have about the topic?	What instruments do you hear?

Name:_____ Date: _____

"Last Dance" by Donna Summer

Lyrics	Music/Accompaniment
What is the song about? Summarize the song.	Describe the music or melody of this song. Is it fast-paced or slow? Does it have low notes or high notes? Is it melodic or does it have lots of percussion?
What are the main points of the song? What is the song saying about the subject?	What feelings do you get from the music? Why?
What mood/values/feelings does the singer have about the topic?	What instruments do you hear?

1. What message do these songs have in common?

   _____

   _____

2. What did disco and disco dancing seem to have provided to people in the 1970s?

   _____

   _____

Name: _____ Date: _____

HANDOUT 9.2
Music in the 1970s
Venn Diagram

Directions: Compare the early 1970s music to disco music using this Venn diagram.

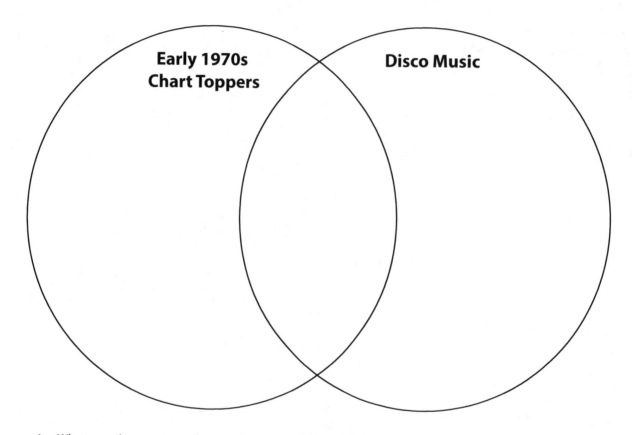

Early 1970s Chart Toppers **Disco Music**

1. What was the message of many disco songs? How did the events in the United States and around the world explain why disco music and disco dancing became so popular at this time?

_____

_____

_____

_____

2. What new experiences or conditions were affecting American identity? How did this explain disco? How did disco and disco dancing fit with the ideas of the "Me Decade" that we talked about earlier in the unit?

_____

_____

_____

_____

LESSON 10

That 70s Show: The 1970s Come to an End

Alignment of Unit Goals

- » Goal 1: To understand the concept of identity in 1970s America.
- » Goal 2: To develop skills in historical analysis and song and artwork interpretation.
- » Goal 4: To develop an understanding of historical events occurring in the United States during the 1970s.

Unit Objectives

- » To describe how the American identity changed during the 1970s.
- » To describe how changes in American identity in the 1970s were revealed in the music, art, and literature of the decade.
- » To define the context in which a song or piece of art was produced and the implications of context for understanding the artifact.

» To describe a writer's or artist's intent in producing a given song or piece of art based on understanding of text and context.

» To describe major historical events during the 1970s that affected the American identity.

» To describe music, art, and literature of the 1970s that reflected the American identity.

Resources for Unit Implementation

» **Handout 10.1:** America in 1979

» **Handout 10.2:** Top 20 Songs in 1979

» **Handout 10.3:** Music Analysis Model (three copies for each student)

» **Handout 10.4:** America in 1979 Identity Chart

» **Listen:** "Tie a Yellow Ribbon Round the Ole Oak Tree" (Levine & Brown, 1973) by Dawn featuring Tony Orlando. Song available on YouTube.

Key Terms

» *Hostage:* a person taken by force and held by another as security for the fulfillment of certain conditions

Learning Experiences

1. To review the 1970s, have students present their Pet Rock projects from Lesson 1. Then, have students complete Handout 10.1 (America in 1979) using what they have learned in this unit. As a whole group, review student responses. **Ask:** Looking at your projects and looking back on what you have learned about the 1970s, what events and people of the 1970s shaped American culture and identity the most? Why do you think this? How uniform do you think America was by the end of the decade? Why?

2. Using your textbook, review the events of 1979. In the fall of 1978, the Shah of Iran, whom the United States supported, was overthrown and the new Ayatollah was hostile to the U.S. In November of 1979, the American embassy in Iran was stormed and 53 Americans were taken hostage due to our support of the Shah. In December, the Soviets invaded Afghanistan and tensions with the Soviet Union increased again. **Ask:** How do you expect Americans responded? Think about what you have studied since World War II. What was the mood of the music you listened to after the dropping of the atomic bomb? What types of songs appeared during the McCarthy hearings? What types of messages did you hear in the music from when the U.S. sent troops into Vietnam? What was the mood of the music about the energy crisis in the early 1970s? Based on what you have seen over the last three decades, what do you expect to see happen now?

3. Play for students "Tie a Yellow Ribbon Round the Ole Oak Tree" (Levine & Brown, 1973) by Dawn featuring Tony Orlando. Tell students that this song was originally released in 1973, but it became popular during the hostage crisis, and people would tie yellow ribbons around trees, fences, and poles during the crisis. **Ask:** What is the mood of this song? What is its message? How does this compare to other music about government actions that you have listened to? Show students the list of Top 20 Songs in 1979 in Handout

10.2. Students can research the lyrics of any songs they do not know. Individually or in small groups, have students complete Handout 10.3 (Music Analysis Model) for at least three songs from the list (make three copies for each student). Discuss their findings. **Ask:** What is the tone and mood of these songs? What are all of these songs about? Are you surprised to find that all of the music is light-hearted? Why are there no songs about the U.S., about international tensions, or about the domestic events going on? What does it tell us about the U.S. in the late 1970s that the only song you see about political events is "Tie a Yellow Ribbon Round the Ole Oak Tree"? Remind students that earlier in the unit, they discussed this as the "Me Decade." Now that the unit is concluding, review the questions posed earlier. **Ask:** What elements of identity became more important to people in the 1970s? Why? How do the political, economic, and social events of the time explain this?

4. Give students an Handout 10.4 (America in 1979 Identity Chart) and have them complete it individually or in small groups by drawing upon everything they have learned in the unit. Discuss student responses as a whole class. **Ask:** Look at Handout 10.1. What does this tell you about America in the 1970s? What does it suggest about the future of the U.S.?

5. Have students write a journal entry as if they were a teenager living in the 1970s. They should imagine it is December 31, 1979, and they are reflecting back on the decade, the things that have happened, and how they feel about them. They also should include their thoughts on the future: What changes do they anticipate? How do they feel about them and what is their outlook for the future? Students should try to stay in the mindset of the 1970s, not today.

Assessing Student Learning

- » Handout 10.1 (America in 1979)
- » Handout 10.2 (Top 20 Songs in 1979)
- » Handout 10.3 (Music Analysis Model)
- » Handout 10.4 (America in 1979 Identity Chart)
- » Discussions

Extending Student Learning

The following are optional activities for extending student learning in this lesson:
- » The yellow ribbon icon is one that still has meaning today. Have students research its origin and its use today in the United States.
- » Have students conduct additional research about the Pet Rock fad, including its origin and the timeline for its appearance in American culture.
- » Students should investigate toys as artifacts from the 1970s. They could research the toys first brought into the American market during the time period.

113

Name: _____ Date: _____

HANDOUT 10.1
America in 1979

Directions: Respond to these questions using what you have learned in this unit.

1. What new ideas and experiences were expressed in the U.S. throughout the 1970s?

   _____

   _____

   _____

2. What new values or priorities were expressed or demanded in the 1970s? How much of a change did these represent for American society?

   _____

   _____

   _____

3. Based on these ideas and experiences, what do you predict for the future of the U.S.? What do you think will happen in the next decade? Will the U.S. change? Why or why not? In what ways?

   _____

   _____

   _____

4. How different are the issues and concerns of the 1970s from the issues and concerns of the U.S. today?

   _____

   _____

   _____

5. Looking at your projects and looking back on what we have learned about the 1970s, what events and people of the 1970s shaped American culture and identity the most? Why do you think this?

   _____

   _____

   _____

Name: _____ Date: _____

HANDOUT 10.2
Top 20 Songs of 1979

Directions: Review this list of the Top 20 Songs of 1979. Select any three, then complete a Music Analysis sheet for each one in Handout 10.3.

1	"My Sharona"	The Knack
2	"Bad Girls"	Donna Summer
3	"Le Freak"	Chic
4	"Do Ya Think I'm Sexy?"	Rod Stewart
5	"Reunited"	Peaches & Herb
6	"I Will Survive"	Gloria Gaynor
7	"Hot Stuff"	Donna Summer
8	"Y.M.C.A."	Village People
9	"Ring My Bell"	Anita Ward
10	"Sad Eyes"	Robert John
11	"Too Much Heaven"	Bee Gees
12	"MacArthur Park"	Donna Summer
13	"When You're in Love with a Beautiful Woman"	Dr. Hook & The Medicine Show
14	"Makin' It"	David Naughton
15	"Fire"	The Pointer Sisters
16	"Tragedy"	Bee Gees
17	"A Little More Love"	Olivia Newton-John
18	"Heart of Glass"	Blondie
19	"What a Fool Believes"	The Doobie Brothers
20	"Good Times"	Chic

HANDOUT 10.3
Music Analysis Model

Directions: After listening to three of the top 20 Songs of 1979, please complete the following music analysis for each selection.

Song Title:_____

What is the title of the song? Why was it given this title?

Title:
Why do you think it was given this title?
Which words in the title are especially important? Why?

What is your reaction to the song?

What is the first thing about this song that draws your attention?
What is in the song that surprises you, or that you didn't expect?
What are some of the powerful ideas expressed in the song?
What feelings does the song cause in you?
What questions does it raise for you?

Handout 10.3: Music Analysis Model, continued

When was the song written? Why was it written?

Who is the songwriter(s)?
When was the song written?
What is the song's purpose? To entertain? To dance to? To critique something?
What were the important events occurring at the time the song was written?
Who is the intended audience?
What biases do you see in the author's lyrics?

What are the important ideas in this song?

Lyrics	Music/Accompaniment
What is the subject of the song? Summarize the song.	Describe the music or melody of this song. Is it fast-paced or slow? Does it have low notes or high notes? Is it melodic or does it have lots of percussion?
What are the main points of the song? What is the song saying about the subject?	What feelings do you get from the music? Why?
What mood/values/feelings does the singer have about the topic?	How does the tone or mood of the music fit with the lyrics? Why might this be?

What is your evaluation of this song?

What new or different interpretation of this historical period does this song provide?
What does this song portray about American identity or how Americans felt at the time?

Name:_____ Date:_____

HANDOUT 10.4
America in 1979
Identity Chart

Directions: Complete this chart using information you have learned in this unit.

Identity changes with new ideas, experiences, conditions, or in response to other expressions of identity.
What new ideas, experiences, technology, conditions, or events came about in the 1970s? How did these change American identity—how Americans did things, what they believed and valued? What traits in America were altered? In what ways? What traits went away? What new traits were added? Why? What issues or developments were still being decided at the end of the decade?

There are multiple elements of identity and at different times, different elements have greater or lesser importance
Which elements of identity became more important through the 1970s? Which elements of identity became less important over the decade?

Handout 10.4: America in 1979 Identity Chart, continued

Although members of a group or society may have different individual identities, they still share particular elements of identity
What group identity emerged by the end of the 1970s—what traits did most Americans share? What elements of identity did Americans still have in common? What divisions existed in American society? What challenges or possibilities faced America as a result?
Summarize the 1970s: How would you describe the 1970s? How do you summarize what the decade was all about?
How have the events of the 1970s shaped our modern American identity and culture?

References

Angelou, M. (2009). *I know why the caged bird sings*. New York, NY: Ballantine. (Original work published in 1969)

Ashford, N., & Simpson, V. (1970). Reach out and touch (somebody's hand) [Recorded by Diana Ross]. On *Diana Ross* [Record]. Detroit, MI: Motown.

Bach, R. (2006). *Jonathan Livingston Seagull*. New York, NY: Scribner. (Original work published in 1970)

Bachman, R. (1975). Lookin' out for #1 [Recorded by Bachman-Turner Overdrive]. On *Head on* [Record]. Chicago, IL: Mercury.

Bee, T. (1972). Beginnings [Recorded by XIT]. On *Plight of the redman* [Record]. Detroit, MI: Motown.

Bee, T. (1973a). Reservation of education [Recorded by XIT]. On *Silent warrior* [Record]. Detroit, MI: Motown.

Bee, T. (1973b). We live [Recorded by XIT]. On *Plight of the redman* [Record]. Detroit, MI: Motown.

Bizeau, B. (1977). Queens of noise [Recorded by The Runaways]. On *Queens of noise* [Record]. Nashville, TN: Mercury.

Brady, J. (1971, December). I want a wife. *Ms.* Retrieved from http://www.columbia.edu/~sss31/rainbow/wife.html

Bridges, A., & Hutcheson, S. (1978). I love the nightlife [Recorded by Alicia Bridges]. On *Alicia Bridges* [Record]. London, England: Polydor.

Burns, B. (1979). Cheaper crude or no more food [Recorded by Bobby Butler]. On *Cheaper crude or no more food* [Record]. Nashville, TN: IBC.

Cash, J., & Cash, J. C. (1974). I'm a worried man [Recorded by Johnny Cash]. On *Ragged old flag* [Record]. New York, NY: Columbia.

Castillo, E., & Kupka, S. (1975). There's only so much oil in the ground [Recorded by Tower of Power]. On *Urban renewal* [Record]. Los Angeles, CA: Warner Brothers.

Center for Gifted Education. (2007). *Guide to teaching social studies curriculum*. Dubuque, IA: Kendall Hunt.

Center for Gifted Education. (2011). *Autobiographies and memoirs*. Dubuque, IA: Kendall Hunt.

David, H., & Bacharach, B. (1969). Raindrops keep fallin' on my head [Recorded by B. J. Thomas]. On *Raindrops keep fallin' on my head* [Record]. New York, NY: Scepter.

Gardiner, D. (1973). President Nixon, don't ration my gas [Recorded by Diana Gardiner]. On *President Nixon, don't ration my gas* [Record]. Retrieved from http://blogfiles.wfmu.org/KF/2006/05/oil/Diana_Gardiner_-_President_Nixon_Don't_Ration_My_Gas.mp3

Gaye, M. (1971). What's going on. On *What's going on* [Record]. Detroit, MI: Motown.

Gaye, M., & Nyx, J. (1971). Inner city blues (make me wanna holler) [Recorded by Marvin Gaye]. On *What's going on* [Record]. Detroit, MI: Motown.

Gibb, B., Gibb, M., & Gibb, R. (1977). Night fever [Recorded by the Bee Gees]. On *Saturday night fever* [Record]. Los Angeles, CA: Reprise.

Gofflin G., King, C., & Wexler, J. (1967). (You make me feel like) a natural woman [Recorded by Carole King]. On *Tapestry* [Record]. Auckland, New Zealand: Ode.

Gonzales, R. (1972). *I am Joaquin*. Retrieved from http://www.latinamericanstudies.org/latinos/joaquin.html

Gordy, B., West, B., Davis, H., & Hutch, W. (1969). I'll be there [Recorded by The Jackson 5]. On *Third album* [Record]. Detroit, MI: Motown.

Harris, T. (2004). *I'm OK—you're OK*. New York, NY: Harper Perennial. (Original work published in 1967)

Hassen, B. (1971). Black is [Recorded by The Last Poets]. On *This is madness* [Record]. New York, NY: Douglas.

Hollein, H. (1972–1982). Abteiberg Museum (Work of architecture). Retrieved from http://hollein.com/eng/Architecture/Nations/Germany/Staedtisches-Museum-Abteiberg

Holler, D. (1968). Abraham, Martin, and John [Recorded by Dion]. On *Dion* [Record]. New York, NY: Laurie.

Huntington, S. P. (2004). *Who are we? The challenges to America's national identity*. New York, NY: Simon and Schuster.

Idelson, G. (2010). 1976 Bicentennial celebration. Retrieved from http://www.savethemall.org/moments/idelson.html

Jabara, P. (1978). Last dance [Recorded by Donna Summer]. On *Thank God it's Friday* [Record]. New York, NY: Casablanca.

Jackson, M., Jackson, D., & Elmar, K. (1978). Blame it on the boogie [Recorded by The Jacksons]. On *Destiny* [Record]. New York, NY: Epic.

Jackson, M., & Jackson, R. (1978). All night dancin' [Recorded by The Jacksons]. On *Destiny* [Record]. New York, NY: Epic.

Joel, B. (1973). Piano man. On *Piano man* [Record]. Los Angeles, CA: Columbia.

Kristofferson, K., & Foster, F. (1969). Me and Bobby McGee [Recorded by Janis Joplin]. On *Me and Bobby McGee* [Record]. New York, NY: Columbia. (1971)

Levine, I., & Brown, R. L. (1973). Tie a yellow ribbon round the ole oak tree [Recorded by Dawn featuring Tony Orlando]. On *Tuneweaving* [Record]. New York, NY: Bell.

Library of Congress. (n.d.). *Using primary sources*. Retrieved from http://www.loc.gov/teachers/usingprimarysources/

McCartney, P. (1970). Let it be [Recorded by The Beatles]. On *Let it be* [Record]. London, England: Apple.

McKeague, P. M. (2009). *Writing about literature* (9th ed.). Dubuque, IA: Kendall Hunt.

Mercury, F. (1977). We are the champions [Recorded by Queen]. On *News of the world* [Record]. London, England: EMI.

Moore, C. (1974–1978). Piazza d'Italia [Work of architecture]. Retrieved from http://www.neworleansonline.com/images/slideshows/listings/1344/05.jpg

National Governors Association Center for Best Practices, & Council of Chief State School Officers. (2010). *Common Core State Standards for English language arts and literacy in history/social studies, science, and technical subjects*. Washington, DC: Authors.

O'Reilly, J. (1971, December). The housewife's moment of truth. *New York*. Retrieved from http://www.nymag.com/news/features/46167

Perren, F., & Fekaris, D. (1978). I will survive [Recorded by Gloria Gaynor]. On *Love tracks* [Record]. Nashville, TN: Polydor.

Reddy, H., & Burton, R. (1971). I am woman [Recorded by Helen Reddy]. On *I don't know how to love him* [Record]. Los Angeles, CA: Capitol.

Reed, J. (1974). The crude oil blues. On *A good woman's love* [Record]. New York, NY: RCA.

Sainte-Marie, B. (1966). My country 'tis of thy people you're dying. On *Little wheel spin and spin* [Record]. New York, NY: Vanguard.

Scarpa, C. (1968–1978). Brion Cemetery [Work of architecture]. Retrieved from http://www.greatbuildings.com/buildings/Brion-Vega_Cemetery.html

Schlafly, P. (1977). *The power of the positive woman*. Retrieved from http://jackiewhiting.net/Women/Power/Schlafly.htm

Simon, C. (1972). You're so vain. On *No secrets* [Record]. Los Angeles, CA: Elektra.

Simon, P. (1970). Bridge over troubled water [Recorded by Simon and Garfunkel]. On *Bridge over troubled water* [Record]. New York, NY: Columbia.

Sinclair, G. (1974). The Americans [Recorded by Byron MacGregor]. On *The Americans* [Record]. Detroit, MI: Westbound.

Smith, A. D. (2010). *National identity (Ethnonationalism comparative perspective)*. Malden, MA: Polity Press.

Springsteen, B. (1975). Born to run. On *Born to run* [Record]. New York, NY: Columbia.

Steinem, G. (1970, August). What would it be like if women win. *Time*. Retrieved from http://www.jackiewhiting.net/AP/Steinmen.htm

Stone, S. (1968). Everyday people [Recorded by Sly and the Family Stone]. On *Stand!* [Record]. New York, NY: Epic.

Taba, H. (1962). *Curriculum: Theory and practice*. New York, NY: Harcourt Brace.

Vonnegut, K. (1999). *Breakfast of champions*. New York, NY: Dial Press. (Original work published in 1973)

Walker, A. (2011). Everyday use. In A. Charters (Ed.), *The story and its writer* (pp. 852–858). Boston, MA: Bedford/St. Martin's. (Original work published in 1973)

Walsh, J. (1978). Life's been good. On *But seriously, folks . . .* [Record]. Los Angeles, CA: Asylum.

Westerman, F. R. C. (1969). Custer died for your sins. On *Custer died for your sins* [Record]. New York, NY: Perception.

Willis, A., & Lind, J. (1979). Boogie wonderland [Recorded by Earth, Wind and Fire]. On *I am* [Record]. New York, NY: ARC/Columbia.

Wonder, S., & Byrd, G. (1976). Black man [Recorded by Stevie Wonder]. On *Songs in the key of life* [Record]. Detroit, MI: Tamla.

Unit Glossary

assassination: the murder of a political figure, often by a surprise attack

bicentennial: a 200th anniversary and/or its celebration

Chicano: initially used as a derogatory term for Mexicans who were born in America and was perceived to be a negative ethnic stereotype. The Chicano Movement used it in a way to show unity among Mexican Americans and pride in their culture.

coalition: a group of people who have joined together to achieve a common purpose

crude oil: a naturally occurring, unrefined petroleum product

civil rights: rights that protect one's individual freedoms within a society

descent: derivation from an ancestor; lineage

disco: popular dance music characterized by a pulsating rhythm, electronically produced sounds, and repetitive lyrics

discrimination: treatment of, or making a distinction in favor of or against, a person based on the group to which the person belongs, rather than on individual merit

embargo: a government order that limits trade in some manner

hostage: a person taken by force and held by another as security for the fulfillment of certain conditions

inflation: a rise in prices related to an increase in the volume of money, resulting in the devaluing of a country's currency

liberation: the seeking of equal status or just treatment for a group believed to be discriminated against

movement: a series of organized activities to obtain an objective

mural: a large picture painted directly on a wall or ceiling

postmodern architecture: a term that is used the describe the architecture of buildings that integrate modernism with some classical or neoclassical elements; the postmodern movement in architecture began in the 1970s

proclamation: an official statement made by a person or people in power

ration: to restrict the distribution and/or consumption of a product

recession: a time of reduced economic activity, varying in scope and duration

self-help: the process of doing things to improve one's self or to solve one's problems without getting help from others

suffrage: the right to vote

# About the Authors

Molly Sandling is a teacher at Jamestown High School in Williamsburg, VA, where she teaches AP U.S. History and AP Human Geography. She completed her bachelor's degree in history at Yale University and her master's degree in education at the College of William and Mary, with an emphasis on adolescent social studies education. While in the master's degree program, she wrote the social studies units *The 1920s in America: A Decade of Tensions*, *The 1930s in America: Facing Depression, Defining Nations*, and *The Renaissance and Reformation in Europe* and received the NAGC Curriculum Award for *The 1920s in America*. Molly has been teaching since 2000 and was the 2010 High School Teacher of the Year for Williamsburg-James City County Public Schools and received National Board Certification in November 2012.

Kimberley Chandler, Ph.D., is the Curriculum Director at the Center for Gifted Education at the College of William and Mary and a clinical assistant professor. Kimberley completed her Ph.D. in Educational Policy, Planning, and Leadership with an emphasis in gifted education administration at the College of William and Mary. Her professional background includes teaching gifted students in a variety of settings, serving as an administrator of a school district gifted program, and providing professional development training for teachers and administrators nationally and internationally. Currently, Kimberley is the Network Representative on the NAGC Board of Directors, Member-at-Large Representative for the AERA Research on Giftedness and Talent SIG, and editor of the CEC-TAG newsletter *The Update*. Her research interests include curriculum policy and implementation issues in gifted programs, the design and evaluation of professional development programs for teachers of the gifted, and the role of principals in gifted education. Kimberley coauthored a book titled *Effective Curriculum for Underserved Gifted Students* and has served as the editor of many curriculum materials (science, social studies, language arts, and mathematics) from the Center for Gifted Education at The College of William and Mary.

Common Core State Standards Alignment

Grade Levels	Common Core State Standards in ELA-Literacy
K-12 College and Career Readiness Anchor Standards	L.CCRA.R.1: Read closely to determine what the text says explicitly and to make logical inferences from it; cite specific textual evidence when writing or speaking to support conclusions drawn from the text.
	L.CCRA.R.2: Determine central ideas or themes of a text and analyze their development; summarize the key supporting details and ideas.
	L.CCRA.R.4: Interpret words and phrases as they are used in a text, including determining technical, connotative, and figurative meanings, and analyze how specific word choices shape meaning or tone.
	L.CCRA.R.7: Integrate and evaluate content presented in diverse media and formats, including visually and quantitatively, as well as in words.
	L.CCRA.R.9: Analyze how two or more texts address similar themes or topics in order to build knowledge or to compare the approaches the authors take.
	L.CCRA.R.10: Read and comprehend complex literary and informational texts independently and proficiently.